GOODBYE TO THE WORKING CLASS

GOODBYE TO THE WORKING CLASS

Roy Greenslade

MARION BOYARS
LONDON

A MARION BOYARS BOOK
Distributed by
Calder & Boyars Ltd
18 Brewer Street, London W1R 4AS

First published in Great Britain in 1976 by
Marion Boyars Publishers Ltd
18 Brewer Street, London W1R 4AS

© Roy Greenslade 1976

ALL RIGHTS RESERVED

ISBN 0 7145 2511 1

Computer typeset by
Input Typesetting Ltd, London SE1
Printed and bound in Great Britain by
REDWOOD BURN LIMITED, Trowbridge & Esher

Acknowledgements

I could not have written this book without the help of many people. My chief debt is, of course, to the one hundred and twenty-two former pupils of Dagenham County High School. Tracking them down would have been impossible without the assistance of Sandra Butcher and Frank Wildman. Thanks are due to the school's headmaster, Frank Grainger, and the chairman of the Board of Governors, Sydney Russell. My research into Dagenham's history would have been indefinitely prolonged without the aid of the local reference librarian, James Howson. I would also like to record my special thanks to five people who offered suggestions on the original draft: Noreen Taylor, Leslie Cannon, Geoffrey Weekes, Enid King and Kay Dick.

Contents

Preface

When my parents were notified in 1958 that I had passed the 11-plus examination their sighs of joy betrayed relief. I was to be spared the four-year 'stretch' at the local secondary modern. It was a glass and concrete building amid an asphalt desert, separated from the surrounding housing estate by a high wire fence. Nobody could mistake it for a concentration camp, a local councillor once commented drily, because there are no watchtowers. The secondary modern, in South Ockendon, Essex, had a reputation for turning bright young minds into dull ones and was never known to trouble university examining boards. This terrifying prospect goes a long way to explaining why my parents were far from alarmed at the thought of my travelling fifteen miles to Dagenham to attend a grammar school. They, and indeed I, may have been comforted by my escape from secondary modern education, but our delight was restrained in comparison with many of the families of my contemporaries who lived in and around Dagenham itself. Secondary modern schools in the area were infamous as training centres for hooliganism and anarchy. For Dagenham children, nurtured like me on the belief that getting to grammar school meant getting on in life, the logical sequence to passing the 11-plus was going to County High. Working class parents wanted their children to have the chance they never had. Winning a place at County High was seen as deliverance from drudgery, the beginning of a straight path to the good life. Blue collar fathers who wished for white collar sons thought their boys were on their way.

One hundred and thirty of us entered the gates of Dagenham County High School aged eleven. We were to find our path littered with obstacles, in the form of examinations, before we emerged into the world. A few obtained university places, others got into college. Most of us went out to work. To the influences of home and school were added those of occupation, possibly marriage. We faced scores of different 'turning points' in the period up to our 26th year. It was at this point – ten years after I left school – that I decided to

1

go back, to track down and talk to all my former school friends. It began as a germ of an idea, implanted one afternoon when an ex-classmate turned up in my office, and grew more sturdily in the weeks after our meeting. He had seen my name in the newspaper, where I worked as a journalist, after arriving to work himself in the same paper's accounts department. Overcome with curiosity he came to see if I was really who he suspected. His curiosity was nothing compared with mine. I began to wonder what had happened to all the others. That journalistic phrase 'Where are they now?' daily ran through my mind, until I could think of nothing else. So I set about tracing the men and women who shared my senior schooldays.

To return to a place which figured for so long in my life produced conflicting sensations. The demolition of a terrace of houses, the erection of high-rise flats, the introduction of a one-way road system, offices where once there was a cinema, an old pub refurbished ... all prompted the thought that 'everything changes'. Then I turned another corner and discovered the same lollipop man on duty at the same school crossing, the same disused hut on the allotment bearing the same graffiti, and the same fish and chip shop in a parade still untouched by neon lighting ... all invoked the opposite feeling – 'nothing changes'. Returning to Dagenham was that sort of confusing emotional cocktail. Just mention of the district is a passport to instant nostalgia. I went to school there for six years and, after leaving, worked for more than three years on one of the local newspapers. As a journalist, if not before, I became intimately involved with the people of Dagenham, Barking and the Becontree Estate. I was on hand to see many political decisions taken, decisions as varied as changing the course of education policy and changing the course of underground sewerage. I reported on industrial matters in one of Britain's biggest car plants. I visited youth clubs, listened to beat groups in garden sheds and spent Hallowe'en round a Scout group camp fire. I went to the schools, to speech days, sports days and open days. I accompanied pensioners on outings. I became an expert at hoop-la because I attended so many garden fêtes. I also saw the other side. I went to magistrates courts. I watched while men were sent to jail, and saw old women weep as they were convicted of shoplifting a half pound of butter. I saw people evicted. I visited children's homes. I was on first-name terms with undertakers and my notebook was sprinkled with reports from the coroner's court. I drank tea and played snooker in the police station. I bought pints for villains in pubs. As an inquisitive, acquisitive observer I thought I knew all there was to know about Dagenham. I could never have been more wrong. Until I went back after six years to meet again those old friends, I shared as many misconceptions about Dagenham and its significance as the people who have never been there and the people who have never been anywhere else.

There can be few more satisfying acts of voyeurism than revisiting former schoolmates to ask them as many questions as you can conceive. I do not wish to claim a prurient motive but to emphasise that I am well aware that nostalgic inquisitiveness has its seamier side. For without doubt it was an amazing experience. To start with I had an arduous job of detection since the school had lost all records. My hit-and-miss method of finding people often led to strange doorstep confrontations which began: 'Hello, it's been a long time. I don't know if you remember me but I know you're . . .' In the end I discovered 128 ex-pupils. Of these, 121 agreed to talk to me. Six refused, and one had been killed some years before in a motor cycle accident.

I remembered a good many names and recognised several faces, but I doubt if I knew 25 very well. In nearly every instance I was warmly received, even though I asked a lot of personal questions, perhaps more searching than any outsider would have dared. I could not have obtained the response I did without some sort of guarantee of anonymity. Therefore, all the names have been changed. Many people will recognise others, or at least think they do. Everyone who took part was aware of this situation and I hope that in taking me into their confidence I can do them justice, even if they remain bewildered by my analysis.

PART ONE

The Setting

Subliminal Schooling

Throughout this century the British have placed their faith in education or, to be more precise, in schooling. It has been eulogised as being the most perfect investment in the country's future by every faction. The capitalist entrepreneur was quick to see the advantage of a skilled work force able to cope with advancing technology. The liberal reformer believed education would prove a great class leveller. The working class saw schooling as an escape route. There was a feeling that 'education' held the key to the future, that it would be the solution to all our ills and, indeed, that without it we would be doomed. H. G. Wells captured that feeling in the 1930s when he wrote: 'Human history becomes more and more a race between education and catastrophe.' [1]

Pressures from all sides for a fairer society culminated in the 1944 Education Act, which dramatically changed the British schooling system in an attempt to offer education for all. Primary schooling was introduced as a separate entity. Fee-paying grammar schools were abolished. A tripartite system of secondary schooling was set up – grammar, technical and modern – and entrance to these was determined by an examination of eleven-year-olds. The course had been set for what was then thought to be equality of opportunity for everyone. However, it soon became clear that secondary selection was crude and cynical. Children good with their heads went to a grammar, those good with their hands to a technical and the rest – the so-called good-for-nothings – were left to the mercy of a modern. Even within the grammar schools there was a noticeable failure to create a climate of equality. Ten years after the Act a government report stated: 'From the children of parents at one (social) extreme to the children of unskilled manual workers at the other there is a steady and marked decline in performance at the grammar school, at the length of school life and in academic promise at the time of leaving.' [2]

In a study carried out during 1952-3 at schools in south-west Hertfordshire and Middlesborough the authors concluded: 'It has now been established beyond doubt that there is a process of social as well as academic selection at work in the schools.' [3] A book published in 1962, *Education and the Working Class,* made a detailed study of the effects of grammar school education in Huddersfield which was based on class inequalities. [4]

Five years later the *Plowden Report,* looking deeper into the problems of low school achievement by working class children in primary schools, stated: 'There is evidence that working class parents have lower educational aspirations than middle class parents, who prefer to have higher occupational aspirations and take more interest in children's progress.' [5]

Reports and studies like these have resulted in gradual changes of direction in schooling, leading to the crumbling of the tripartite system, the ending of 11-plus selection and the formation of comprehensive schools. What investigations have not taken account of is the form of education offered by the schools and the results of that education. Research has illuminated the social inequality evident in classrooms but has cast no light on the type of person who emerges from the educational system. Jackson and Marsden did make an attempt at showing what happened to grammar school leavers, asking whether working class children gained or lost in achieving middle class status. It was a loaded question with a built-in preconception about the nature of social mobility. Do working class children really enter the middle class? The authors also chose the 'cream', those people who passed GCE A–level, and accepted the winning of university degrees as a 'success'. They spoke of the system's inability to move the bulk of working class children into higher education as 'a colossal waste of talent'. [6] None of these eccentricities is as bad as their blind acceptance of the fact that Britain's education, if made freely available to all classes, is acceptable as it stands. Here is a real lack of objectivity. School is not a neutral agent in the influences it has over children in spite of the home being the dominant power. Whether the school provides a different environment from home or not, it plays a vital role in the child's growing-up process. In fact, school as the reinforcement of parental values is yet more influential than if it offers a totally opposite culture rather like the Press, which by its subtle maintenance of support for the status quo, exercises subliminal control over society. Both schools and newspapers, incidentally, boast of being free and open.

As a working class child in a working class area I admit that our grammar school was open in the sense that we did not have to compete with the middle class to enter. However, this 'free and open' education did not leave me believing the working class should have more of it. Just the reverse. I maintain that it was several years, and by considerable chance, before I overcame the effects of that education, if indeed I have done so. The schooling offered to us was so closed, so enslaving and therefore dangerous, that I consider it one small example of a large-scale crime.

In this study, I asked a set of straightforward questions with which I hoped to prompt a discussion. That I rarely achieved more than a disjointed nostalgic talk is evidence of the disquieting situation I discovered. My aim was to find out what sort of people my contemporaries are now; what makes them tick; and why they are what they are. I begin with a look at the unique area of Dagenham, followed by a personal retrospective view of Dagenham County High School. In Part Two are the interviews. I start with a look at the parents and their various attitudes before meeting their children. I have dealt separately with the working and middle classes because that is the best way to illustrate the class chasm into which our education system is pitching an ever-increasing number of people. In the third chapter of this section I take a closer look at three people whose personal stories are of wider interest than the general thesis; and in the fourth I examine three aspects of behaviour – speech and literacy, the use of drugs, and sexual attitudes. My conclusion forms the final section.

Landscape for a Working Class

Dagenham is a planner's nightmare and a sociologist's dream. It is a working class colony without equal. Its dominating features are the Ford car plant and the Becontree Estate, the biggest housing estate in Britain.[1] Twenty-seven thousand houses built to the same monotonous pattern — two-storey, terraced, rust-bricked, uniformly-painted, small-windowed, narrow-gardened. The similarity overawes, and pathetic attempts at road layout gimmickry fail to relieve its monolithic quality. The area is also flat, so flat that one school friend told me he was eleven before he discovered that all hills didn't have trains running underneath. The topography may partly excuse the planners, but they must have learned their lesson for never again have they constructed a housing eyesore to match Becontree.

Before the builders arrived Dagenham was a quite agricultural village, 'an obscure crossroads' just beyond better-known Barking.[2] It is more than a little ironic that Charles Dickens should have chosen the Essex marshes surrounding Dagenham as the setting for the opening scene of his novel *Great Expectations*. For the expectations of both Dagenham and its inhabitants have never justified the superlative. Greatness should not be thrust upon Dagenham. Even the history books chronicle it as an appendage to Barking, although both places are recorded as early Saxon settlements bearing the names Daeccanham (Daecca's village) and Berecingum (Berica's people). It was Barking that was chosen in AD 666 by St Erkenwald, the Bishop of London, as the site for an abbey for his sister Ethelburga. Its so-called remoteness was considered to provide safety from the Danes but nobody explained that view to the Norsemen who in AD 870 burned the abbey to the ground and killed its inmates. The abbey was rebuilt nearly a hundred years later and once the Normans arrived Barking Abbey was confirmed in all its possessions by William the Conqueror. So the surrounding manors, including Dagenham, flourished under royal patronage for 200 years. Kings, however, play a lesser role in

10

Dagenham's history than the Thames. In 1377 the river and its tiny tributary, the Beam, burst their banks and flooded some of the richest arable land between Barking and Dagenham. Hastily constructed flood walls failed to stop the rivers overflowing again soon after and the spreading waters began to drain away the abbey's finances. This decline was completed by Henry VIII in 1539 during the dissolution and two years later the Saxon building was a ruin. The manors then changed hands at court like Monopoly property cards and all attempts at draining the land failed. A disastrous flood in 1707 left one thousand acres of Dagenham land under water and schemes to construct defences were thwarted by some skilful embezzlement of funds and less than skilful application to the engineering problems involved.

The fact that Dagenham Breach, as it became known, lay upstream on the nation's greatest commercial river guaranteed that it would not remain a watery waste. The impetus of the Industrial Revolution caused London to spread eastwards, so that by 1855 the Royal Victoria Dock was opened just a few miles from Dagenham, and one speculator saw his chance. Samuel Williams, a Victorian businessman of self-made, self-help stock, devised a simple plan to fill in the Breach, his barges carrying downriver excavated soil from the Underground system then being built in the City to be dumped on the Dagenham marshland. A quay wall was constructed and by 1894 the remarkable Mr Williams had filled more than thirty acres of marsh. An Essex backwater was on the brink of industrial transformation. As the Williams' company prospered a jetty was built at what was called, as it still is, Dagenham Dock. Land reclamation continued and between 1909-14 four factories were erected on what was once bog. The dock grew in importance and the arrival of steam power, which turned Dagenham's once rural riverside into bustling activity, had the opposite effect on the fishermen of Barking creek, where the port was shut down.

By 1921 Dagenham's new-found industry, along with more intensive market gardening, supported a population of just over 9,000. It was around this time that London County Council officials walked eastwards out of the capital until they reached the first big open space of Barking and Dagenham. They thought they had hit upon the at-a-stroke solution to their housing headache. Conditions in East End tenements were noted with masterly understatement by the LCC as 'generally the worst' in London, and there was great pressure on the council and the government. After the Great War for freedom, thought the planners, let's build a

11

Great Housing Estate for people to enjoy that freedom. Three thousand acres of land were purchased and the Becontree Estate grew up over a twelve-year period. In 1933 almost 90,000 people lived in Dagenham.

The early Estate residents were the first to suffer the now-familiar anxieties of people moved wholesale in city centre clearance schemes and transported miles to 'nice, new homes' in the countryside. Most of them were prosperous working class families, as Terence Young pointed out: 'The people of the Becontree Estate are not what is generally termed "slum people" ... most slum dwellers could not afford the rents.' [3] Many men were dockers, printers and building workers. Later Ford's and new local industry attracted a lot of the skilled and semi-skilled labour from the Estate.

I have been careful to mention the Becontree Estate as distinct from Dagenham because here lies one of the district's major problems of identification. The Estate also has large sections in Barking and Ilford and formed, in 1961 for example, under half of Dagenham Borough's total housing, the rest being local council or private property. [4] Dagenham grew up alongside and because of Becontree, with its own estates which originally helped take the Estate's 'overspill' – the young people who met and married. When saturation was reached, thousands of sons and daughters left the area, taking another stage further the decline of the 'extended family' of London's East End which itself began with the move to Dagenham. Willmott says the local council were forced to provide an overspill estate twenty miles to the east at Canvey Island and quotes one Dagonian as saying: 'It's a ridiculous situation. The LCC puts its overflow into Dagenham. Dagenham puts its overflow, of necessity, out to Canvey Island. Where they go from Canvey Island in the next generation, God knows. We can only assume they'll put them on rafts and set them adrift.' [5] It is not merely the political and economic interdependence of Becontree and Dagenham that causes confusion. Visitors faced with the repetitive mass of houses and a lack of boundary signs never know exactly which borough they are in. To them, it's all Dagenham.

Another myth is that the Becontree Estate was raised by order of the Ford Motor Company. Journalists have long written of Dagenham in articles on Ford's as if they are one and the same. John G. O'Leary[6], the then borough librarian, raged in his 1962 annual report: 'What do they know of Dagenham who only the Ford works know? We have had of late a rare Press show. Journalists (the sort that print their names under their columns)

12

have looked at Ford's, at the Ford workers, drunk beer in the pubs with them and have set down their impressions of it all whether they know it or not. Their judgements on Dagenham are like an opinion on Indonesia voiced by a traveller who has spent two hours on the airfield at Djakarta.'

Not only reporters make the error. A Yorkshire friend who spent two hours on the Estate later told me: 'I thought Bradford was end o' world 'til I cum 'ere. It's like bluidy Ford barracks.'

Even residents, wrongly believing that Ford employs almost every man in the area, have an inflated opinion of the factory's worth. Said one: 'Take Ford's away and Dagenham would be a ghost town.'

What must be made clear is that the houses arrived first with Henry Ford a close second. Like Samuel Williams, Ford foresaw the importance of the Dagenham marshland. With a businessman's eye he surveyed the site — undeveloped and ripe for expansion; next to the Thames, a cheap way to import raw materials and export the finished product; next door to London, Britain's largest single market; and next to the growing Becontree Estate, a vast pool of labour. Engineering experts said it was impossible to build a factory on the marshes but Ford, like the visionary Victorian before him, was not to be dissuaded and 27,000 concrete piles put his car factory on a firm foundation. In October 1931 the Dagenham plant purred into life and, as Henry predicted, it just went on expanding so that by the early 1960s Ford was employing 55,000 workers there.[7]

The Ford works is a town within a town. It has its own power station, foundry forge, blast furnace and wharf. It has its own road and rail network. The police force and fire brigade are Ford's own. The factory is constantly humming, with an assembly line churning out 1,600 cars every day. If the Becontree Estate is offending to the eye in its unending similarity then the Ford foundry is yet more offensive to the ear and nose. It is impossible to talk below a shout and the stench is unforgettable. Worse still is the monotony of assembly line work. The man who sat at a machine inserting bits of metal one after the other throughout his shift is still the most poignant memory of a school trip round the plant. So many of us emerged from the factory gates that day and vowed never to re-enter.

Another persuasive Press fable linking Ford's factory with the surrounding estates has been that every other Dagenham house has a Red in bed. The local branch of the Communist Party would have been gratified if it was so. In fact, the main conflict at Ford's

13

in the late Fifties and early Sixties was a trial of strength between management and shop stewards, few of whom were communistic in outlook or practice. These men were elected by shop floor workers as protection against the bosses, and they certainly needed a measure of defence as the company strove for higher production efficiency. A war of attrition among stewards and lower management – foremen and supervisors – caused many stoppages and culminated in a Court of Inquiry after a steward was sacked.[8] The inquiry revealed that the shop stewards were financed independently of their unions and acted without central union advice or permission. They were, said the report, 'a union within a union'. Six years later another Court of Inquiry[9] upheld the company's right to employ, and seventeen sacked men remained outside the gates. It was to break the strength of the shop stewards. The legend persists that the stewards were controlled by Communists, but I find it most unlikely. According to Huw Beynon 'the Communist Party had a branch based upon the Dagenham estate with about 100 members.'[10] My dealings with the Communist Party during my years as a local reporter suggest that members tended to boast of more power than in truth they had. A Communist candidate stood in Dagenham at every general election but he polled few votes and the Labour Party count it as one of their safest seats. At local level, Labour's only political opposition of worth stems from the Ratepayers' Association, and that in only one ward of private housing.

Dagenham's population was, in 1961, 108,368 and the overwhelming majority were working class. Leslie Cannon, now the deputy librarian of Barking, says: 'It's probably the most solidly working class district in the world – including Moscow.'[11] Once those workers were settled into their homes – and Ford had conquered the marshes – scores of company bosses moved into the area, offering the residents jobs closer to home. Dagenham had become a capitalist paradise, with employers reaping the benefits of a passive working population. The workers' environment, however, fell far short of the standard set by the Garden of Eden. Dagenham had two vast parks and five smaller ones, which all shared the unfortunate fate of being as flat as billiard tables. In soccer-crazy Dagenham there was no better feature than level grass and all parks were fully used at weekends as the local youth competed for various championships and trophies. I recall many frosty Sunday mornings at Central Park with scores of teenagers changing in wooden huts to play before a cluster of giggling girlfriends and partisan parents. There was a singular attention to football. No

14

other sport, not cricket, tennis, golf, boxing, nor swimming generated such an interest. An ingenious council-sponsored activity known as the Playleader Scheme kept children off street corners during evenings and holidays. There was also a well-patronised network of youth clubs, and Scouting boomed. At the other end of the age range, the elderly were well catered for with old peoples' clubs. These Darby and Joan groups met each week, usually in draughty halls, for a cup of tea, a chat and often a sing-song. Outings were organised, parties were planned and self-help schemes were formulated. One of my first reporting assignments was to accompany old folks on an outing and I was struck by two points I was later to discover were the hallmark of all such clubs in Dagenham. First, the atmosphere of good humour. Second, all the men and women were traditional working class. Admittedly, it was a working class area but in few other groups was there such a noticeable mono-class representation, and never was I subjected to a similar battering of class jingoism – men fiercely proud of having worked thirty years at East Ham gas works, women recalling hard but happy times as children in the heart of the East End.

Young and old were looked after in the community, but what about the workers? There was little interest in cultural pursuits, although Dagenham Libraries Department did its best to foster a drama group, choral society and discussions. Mr O'Leary, the chief librarian, knew attendances were poor and the commitment was small but he felt it warranted. He wrote in 1963: 'Dagenham and the arts. What's being done? Something modest, but something.' The three cinemas did not draw large crowds. Church going was unpopular. [12] Television kept most people at their firesides because even the pubs were uninviting. [13] Most were built on gigantic lines, cavernous echo chambers with all the intimacy of an aircraft hangar. Unloved as they were by many residents, they found favour with the young. The vast pre-war Merry Fiddlers provided a nightly opportunity for unsuspecting drinkers to be deafened by a pop group, soaked in their own beer by a jostling crowd, and frustrated by an inability, on finally returning to the bar, to get served. The Church Elm, constructed on similar barn-like principles, had at one time the dubious distinction of possessing the longest public bar in Greater London. Pub-going was very much part of the growing-up process for adolescents. Downing your first pint was as important as kicking a football straight and kissing a girl in the back seat of the cinema.

Before I set foot in Dagenham I was warned of the dangers lurking in the evening shadows ... razor gangs, bully boys and demon drunks. The area presented a violent image to the outside world, few believing that so many working people could live in harmony. Residents who should have known better gossiped about hooliganism and brawls. In truth, there was some vandalism. Violence was less easy to monitor. I believe there was an aura of restrained violence, a nagging thought that it might erupt given the correct set of conditions. Most incidents tended to be low-key, as one ex-County High pupil described: 'If I went too far out of my own area, around Halbutt Street, even down to Oxlow Lane, then I'd be questioned by a gang. I remember them as teddy boys, but it was probably after that era. I got punched a few times but it wasn't that so much as the humiliation of being restricted.' Another, who lived outside Dagenham, said he often heard stories of fights though he never actually witnessed one. What he did see, he said, were 'louts standing near the Heathway Station'. Some spoke of being scared to walk around at night; others recalled fictionalised fights between gangs. There was not, however, the organised gang complex these quotes suggest. Said one girl: 'Teachers at secondary moderns went in fear because of threats from older boys.' Telephones in kiosks were always out of order, remarked another. There were certainly a few scuffles after school between County High boys and those from the neighbouring secondary modern, Beverley. These 'set battles' occurred infrequently and listening to accounts ten years later I realised how legends are born. The Metropolitan Police Office could not give figures for violent crime in Dagenham, but a helpful Station Sergeant did say: 'Violence here is worse than we would wish but not as bad as everyone thinks.'

One of the great contradictions about people's opinions on Dagenham was that, in spite of the so-called violent society, there were many whose first reaction to the question: 'What did you think of Dagenham?' was to say how friendly the area was. Much of this feeling derived from the East End culture. One who had left said: 'Working class people communicate more easily, and because it was a one-class place there was an openness. It had no pretensions.'

Another, who has stayed, said: 'What a great project to house all those people. It has more friendliness, and more amenities than anywhere else.' A woman who made the unusual move from Dagenham further into East London said: 'I like Dagenham people, East End people. It may not look nice but all I know is that I'd rot in Wickford.' [14]

Some, with nostalgic affection, recalled happy youth in the

16

streets and parks; and a few considered it a good place to be a teenager. Hindsight, and a developed perspective, produced a crop of laconic descriptions about Dagenham. 'Dirty and squalid', said one; 'depressing and soulless', said another; 'an inhuman eyesore,' another.

People who have moved far away from Dagenham – to the North for example – were able to compare it with highly industrialised cities, and it is their comments, perhaps, which are more valid. One man, now lecturing at Sheffield University and living in Barnsley, considered Dagenham much more prosperous than most of South Yorkshire. But, during his schooldays, he hated the area because of its monotonous housing uniformity. Through his Tory father's propaganda he thought that Dagenham was the image of socialism – equality with drabness – but the poverty in parts of Barnsley and Sheffield had changed his views.

Another who lived in Yorkshire, said: 'There are naturally worse places than Dagenham ... towns and cities that have grown up over centuries and then been forced into the industrial revolution. These have worse conditions than any I saw in Dagenham. But Dagenham was planned only forty years ago – as such it's a disgrace. It's oppressive and repressive.'

Those who have gone to largely rural areas, where the rolling green pastures, grazing cattle and slower pace of life have made Dagenham appear like a built-up, industrial nightmare, were equally condemnatory. One woman now living in the Welsh countryside, obviously asked the same question before, said in a robot-like monotone: 'Utilitarian. Dirty. Smoky. Grimy.'[15] That view was echoed by many others who travelled only twenty or so miles away from Dagenham into mid-Essex. One said: 'Did you notice the constant hum of factories? It's great to escape from that.'

However unfair those views may be – Dagenham cannot after all change its location – none was more revealing than this, which gets right to the heart of what many people think of the area. Said one interviewee: 'I enjoyed myself in Dagenham when I was young but I never admit now that I come from there.'

Few were candid enough to say that Dagenham was on 'the wrong side of the tracks'. But I am convinced that a lot of them secretly hold that opinion.

17

High School, or Low?

When the British introduced into their language the term 'grammar school' they could not have been aware that one day it would lead to Dagenham County High School. Grammar schools were originally places 'for the learning of Latin and Greek grammar'.[1] At County High, there were no lessons in Greek and the learning of Latin was the foremost consideration of few pupils and fewer parents. It suggested a return to the past, and working class parents looked to the school to give us children a better future.

County High, built in the heart of the Becontree Estate, was Dagenham's first secondary school when it opened in September 1936. In spite of the borough's 40,000 school-age population, the new grammar school began life with just 90 scholars, four members of staff and a headmaster. The building was so large that Miss Dora Williams, then senior mistress teaching music and Latin, was to remark later that 'visitors left convinced there were no pupils'. Miss Williams, who became head of the school after the war until 1955, died aged 78 in July 1973. In 1957, on the school's 21st anniversary, she wrote a short appreciation of the school in its magazine which clearly shows how Dagenham children regarded – or were taught to regard – their massive new centre of learning.

'Those first pupils set a standard for themselves and their successors. No foot must be set on the footrests of the library tables, no mark made on the spotless walls, no book or article of clothing left lying about its classrooms or cloakrooms ... I fear it was the war that lowered those standards.'

During 1939 the school was evacuated to Norfolk, but the building itself was opened a year later to provide some sort of grammar schooling for those children from surrounding areas who were not evacuated. Miss Williams took over the job of head, and part of the daily routine for pupils was to act as rooftop spotters for 'buzz bombs'. When the war was over the school settled down, though footrests were scuffed, walls were marked and odd bits and pieces could be found stowed in many a corner. In 1956, Mr F. L.

Grainger, who had previously taught history at Dagenham County High, became headmaster. It was under him that I and all the other people in this survey spent our years at the school.[2]

County High meant many things to different people, as I discovered during my research, and my view is coloured by the same half-forgotten fiction, apocryphal fantasy and romantic notion as the rest. However, I will attempt as objective an appraisal as possible of life in the school during the late Fifties and early Sixties, weaving in a little nostalgia.

County High taught about 600 pupils at a time during the years I attended. Classes were about 30-35 in strength and usually there were three forms of each age-group, but ours was a unique intake and there were four. There was intense pressure on all secondary schools in 1958, because it was the culmination of what educationists call the 'bulge year' and what population experts refer to as the 'demographic hump', the birth period which occurred in Britain in 1946-47 roughly nine months after the end of World War Two. County High, like many other schools, was forced to offer more places, and although records have been lost, it appears that 133 started in that term – the school's highest intake. The pressures on classroom space created problems, part of which were solved by turning a small section at the back of the hall, under the balcony, into an open-plan classroom. It was the reverse of the situation in 1936 when the school had 90 pupils.

The school was designed to meet the growing interest in the teaching of science subjects and had laboratory-classrooms for physics, chemistry and biology. Catering for other specialist subjects, there were rooms for domestic science, woodwork, art and music. The curriculum also included – though not for all – French, Latin and German; geography and history; religious knowledge; and, of course, mathematics and English. There was a gymnasium, with showers and changing rooms for boys and girls; and a library. This was a large, wood-panelled room with long, polished desks and book-filled shelves. It had an aura of learning about it. The selection of books was wide; the collection of journals and newspapers was always kept up to date; and the rule of silence was well observed.[3]

The school adopted the rather strange practice of creating six days out of five. The school rota was arranged on a six-day cycle so that Monday's lessons in the first week of term were not repeated until Tuesday of the second week and Wednesday of the third and so on. Confusing as it may sound, it seemed to work well enough.

County High, being the borough's only grammar school, was the subject of many conflicting emotions among the local people, from respect to suspicion and on to hostility. The latter was prevalent, naturally, among those whose sons and daughters failed the 11-plus, but it was equally noticeable in the parents of some who passed. More commonly, the parents were suspicious of the school. They were aware that their offspring were entering an alternative environment and would be open to a different set of values – maybe a new culture. This wariness led many to over-react to school decisions and to question school discipline. The most common parental anxiety was over homework. School, for them, had begun and ended at the school gates; they were genuinely concerned about the totality of a grammar school education. It tempered their delight at their particular child 'making it'. One father said: 'When he went to County High I thought he'd done it all. He'd just have to float along. I never pushed him at home because it didn't seem right.' A mother, living on the Becontree Estate, said: 'Both my children went to County High. I thought it was great at first but they had to work so hard. I went up to see the headmaster about it.' That sentence recurred scores of times during my interviews, from both pupils and parents, and was acknowledged by the headmaster, Mr Grainger. He said: 'Dagenham parents just didn't understand the grammar school principle. We were put in the position year after year of educating the parents rather than their children.'

On occasion, parental worry could not be assuaged, tempers flared and uneasy compromises were reached, making the pupil's daily school life a little more difficult to bear. At home, the pupil would be subjected to tirades of resentment against the school; at school, the pupil would have to put out of his mind the fireside rebellion and try to conform. Intolerable as this must have been there was no parent-teacher association, the much-vaunted modern way to break down the barriers of communication. True, the headmaster's door was always open to parents, but for every one who took advantage of it, there would be another who would not, perhaps being overawed or even apathetic.

The initial intrusion for parents was the purchasing of a uniform . . . a black blazer, a cap or beret, a tie, sports kit and miscellaneous items like scarves and socks and satchels and summer frocks and soccer boots, all labelled with name tags. They felt exploited by having to go to the school's selected outfitters and paying prices they, rightly or wrongly, felt were higher than elsewhere. For some it was undoubtedly a financial burden and a real sacrifice. For a few it was an impossibility and their children were never equipped in County High's sombre black, blue and white. It is not, however, fair to say that they suffered unduly for deviating from the uniform. Apart from infrequent purges by one or two eccentric members of staff the regulations concerning dress were not enforced rigidly. Caps were discarded very quickly, within a month of starting in most cases, and were certainly never worn by anybody above the second year. There was the odd boy who wore jeans to school, but it was extremely rare; nearly all wore the black jackets; most sported grey trousers and the regulation tie. Sweaters were multi-coloured in winter – and teachers rarely questioned offenders. This fairly relaxed attitude on the boys' side was not so on the girls'. They had to wear berets throughout their school careers and were closely watched for attempts to introduce fashion into uniform. This attention to detail was not paid to girls with needy parents. Many of the girls I spoke to were surprisingly irate about the uniform regulation, though most favoured it. The great majority of boys thought uniform a good idea.

In our first year at school we were arbitrarily deposited in four classes, and told that our position in Christmas term and Summer term examinations would decide our stream the following year. How could you convince children at twelve that the two examinations they faced that year were yet more important than the one at eleven which they had been so brainwashed to believe was life's most important? What backing from parents could pupils expect when as far as parents were concerned they had 'made it' already? This lack of parental understanding can be closely related to backgrounds. Many pupils were unprepared for the race. While some were breasting the tape others were inspecting the starting blocks. This system of segregation was to upset a lot of boys and girls and was, in a few cases, so keenly felt that when I spoke to them fourteen years later it was their main memory of school.

(Not so me, I must admit. That first year at County High ended in a glorious summer. I recall watching the sixth formers playing crown and anchor for half-a-crown stakes in the bushes at the side of the canteen during the inter-house cricket matches. I remember the shirt-sleeved choir singing the Hallelujah Chorus from Handel's *Messiah*; and the gush of titters as the sexiest girl prefect in living history engaged in a passionate kiss in the school's presentation of *Antigone*. I recollect a youth in a wheelchair being guest of honour at the sports day; he had been the school's and the county's champion athlete until stricken by polio. That one term is more vivid in my memory than any other.)

At the start of the second term we were herded into our

21

respective streams A, B, C, and D. And so the divisions began. The top three streams took Latin; the D class did not. In the third year the A stream learned German; the others did not. Very laudable, said one educationist I spoke to. It must have given the slower learners the chance to catch up in the mainstream subjects. If that was the idea then the school did not set about it the right way, for the majority view in the survey was that the A stream got the best teachers – and the best breaks. And none of the interviewees disputed that the D stream, with one or two exceptions, got the less competent staff.

An illustration of the streaming system at its worst was the preoccupation with providing teachers at all costs for the top classes, particularly the A group. When a teacher, say, for the A class was away ill, the B teacher would move up, the C would move up to B, and the D up to C, leaving the D class with what was termed 'a revision period' without supervision. That class was probably the least likely of all to work without pressure and so such periods were not noted for their devotion to things academic. If that was bad it does not match the cynicism of the mathematics teacher who in the GCE examination year allowed his D group pupils to read comics if they preferred, as long as they kept quiet during his lessons. Every D class pupil I interviewed – and there were 20 – remembered this point. It is not without significance that of those 20 no less than 17 came from council accommodation. In the other three classes the division between children from private and council housing was much more evenly spread, though since the great majority came from council houses all classes were dominated by them. I also ought to add that the fact that many D class pupils later passed GCE exams was a triumph of will over the system.

To return then to the year by year progress. Once we reached the end of the third year we were asked, at about fourteen years of age, to make the most difficult decision of our lives up to that point. We had to choose which eight subjects we would take at GCE O–level. We were to segregate ourselves – into scientists or artists, linguists or economists. Everyone had to take mathematics, English language, English literature, and one science. The other four subjects were open to choice. This crossroads was met with humour or with anxiety, but however it was faced, many were later to regret their decision. To some extent the choice ended the streaming, though it continued in maths and English. However, the die had been cast; two years in form A gave pupils much more confidence than their colleagues in C or D. The eight GCE subjects system was criticised by a few ex-pupils, but in the main won praise. The headmaster surprised me by saying he would have liked to have seen only six subjects taken at O–level – leaving more time to concentrate on humanities and the arts. 'It was,' said Mr Grainger, 'one of the problems of grammar school that pupils were there to pass exams. It left no time for a wider education.' That statement would have surprised many other pupils too who commented at length on the pressures they felt because of the need to pass examinations. For them, and me, the headmaster embodied our fears if we did not measure up to the task. It was strange that none of us knew his feelings on the matter at the time.

Nobody I spoke to during my study ever mentioned getting close to the headmaster, and with 600 pupils in the school personal relationships would have been impossible with all. He played safe, showing no favour to an individual, and won a reputation for aloofness and – since he was the final arbiter in matters of discipline – as a strict disciplinarian. It was a description he was quick to dispute when I told him. 'I never tried to be high and mighty,' he said, coincidentally choosing the very phrase which scores of ex-pupils had used to describe him. And with that contradiction I think there the matter should rest.

What is less easily explained is the communication barrier that existed between the staff and the pupils. Some teachers were praised for achieving discipline; for teaching with humour; for simply doing their job well. Some were criticised for not achieving discipline; for being humourless; for doing their job badly. None were given credit for being especially friendly, except in one instance. (One boy, from a poor background and with a knack of getting into trouble, was shown exceptional understanding by his form master.) The rarity of that case made me aware of the isolation of teaching staff, and without claiming that it was an unfriendly school I think there was a measurable distance between the boys and girls and the masters and mistresses. This applied, by the way, only until the sixth form, where, as we shall see later, pupils found such a difference in their treatment and relationships with staff they wondered if they had changed schools. It perfectly illustrates the invisible barrier that existed for the first five years. Paradoxically, Mr Grainger said: 'Other headmasters may have run schools more efficiently but none was happier than ours.' I can only believe that the staff laughed a lot in private . . .

Co-educational schools have a duality of standard in their treatment of the two sexes which makes it amusing to watch in practice. Someone, somewhere had obviously to decide where to draw the lines – where the mixing had to stop and the segregation to begin. At County High, the classes were mixed and so were the dinner tables in the canteen. But each sex had their own playground. The girls took domestic science; the boys did woodwork. Physical education was segregated. Boys in trouble were referred to the headmaster; girls to the headmistress. Boy prefects had their own room and so did the girls. The split was the same for the staff, male and female teachers each having their own staffroom. With perhaps two exceptions the staff – both male and female – also addressed the sexes differently. Boys were referred to by their surnames and girls by their Christian names. No pupil ever questioned the status quo and the divisions were accepted without a murmur. Another anomaly crops up here: in the sixth form boys were allowed to take up cookery and the girls were not allowed to do woodwork. I was among several boys who produced a lemon meringue flan and a Christmas cake.

Except for a group of boys from the Richard Alibon Junior School all pupils arrived at County High from co-educational primary schools and there was no marked hostility between sexes. There were, naturally, three-day crushes, two-week romances, and one-month love affairs, some of which would be accompanied by sighing and crying and threats of dying. On the boys' side there tended to be lots of boasting and on the girls' a great deal of blushing but most liaisons were harmless, and very few distracted enough for schoolwork to suffer more than temporarily. Only one girl was forced to leave because of pregnancy. There are no national statistics with which to compare, but the number of inter-school marriages, after leaving, was, I thought, remarkably high. Out of the 122 interviewees, there were four couples from our one year; two more boys married girls in lower forms; three girls married boys from upper forms; and another girl married a boy one year her junior . . . ten inter-marriages in all. There can be little better illustration of the peaceful co-existence of sexes.

County High School was situated at the edge of a huge park, Parsloes, in the middle of the Dagenham portion of the Becontree Estate. It was not peculiarly well placed for transport, but it drew its pupils from long distances. Apart from serving the Estate and Dagenham, pupils travelled from Barking in the east; from Ilford and Hainault in the north; from Romford, Hornchurch and Upminster in the west; and from the Thameside areas of Rainham, Elm Park and Purfleet. A few travelled even more prodigious distances – from South Ockendon, Tilbury and Benfleet. And two of us, in our last three years at the school, did a daily 50-mile round trip from Leigh-on-Sea. This journey, I hasten to add, was of our

24

own choosing. We were offered, and rejected, transfer to a local school when our families moved house.

The breakdown of home locations of the 122 interviewees, when at school, was as follows: 64 lived in Dagenham; 9 in Barking; 6 in Ilford; 4 in Romford; and 9 in Rainham and Elm Park. All those were neighbouring districts. The most popular areas after these were Hornchurch where 11 lived, and Upminster with 7. Five travelled from South Ockendon, 2 from Tilbury and 1 from Purfleet. One boy lived in Hutton; one girl travelled from Benfleet, and 2 came from Leigh-on-Sea.

The District Line Underground trains from Upminster to Dagenham Heathway were a main link and the Tilbury line to Dagenham Dock was another. The most difficult trip was probably from the south west side of the council estate at South Ockendon. Pupils had to take a bus to the station, catch a notoriously inefficient branch line train to Upminster and continue by Underground to the Heathway station. Once there, and this was one of the area's main route centres, they would join scores of boys and girls waiting to get the one bus – the London Transport 148 route – that went to the school. Queues for buses to school in the morning were crowded with County High pupils, but they were orderly. Returning home in the afternoon, however, bus conductors found themselves besieged at the bus-stop outside the school by pushing, yelling boys using bulging satchels like gladiatorial maces. The fight to get home was never pretty. What's more the trip was free for most who used the bus, their fares being paid by the local authority.

The widespread intake was common to all years in the school and was the policy of the controlling authority, the Essex County Council. The 11-plus examination was not simply a straight split between grammar and secondary modern school. Some children who passed chose, or were given, a technical education, a schooling designed to offer practical and handiwork subjects. More complex still was the grammar school division, the subtleties of which were not made public. However, parents, especially among the middle class and the 'aspiring' working class, became aware of what was a 'good' or 'bad' grammar school. The County High headmaster admitted to me that his school was 'in the second division'. A couple of ex-pupils thought it third rate. What became evident in several interviews was that many people were surprised they got to grammar school at all, and others said they were probably borderline 11-plus passes. These usually came from the districts outside Dagenham, for the opinions of Dagenham children, and

25

their parents, were quite different. Dagenham parents were generally proud of their children's achievement and wanted them to go to the local grammar. Therefore, most of the indigenous population made County High their first choice; but those outside the area, in just about every case, were surprised by going to Dagenham. It was a simple case of the authorities fulfilling the requirement. There were not enough Dagenham boys and girls to fill the school so others were brought in to make up the numbers. These were, naturally, the borderline 11-plus passes who had been rejected by the first division grammar schools in their own areas which creamed off the brightest pupils.

Apart from the pupils accepted after the 11-plus, County High also took in about 20 pupils who passed the 13-plus examination. These people were placed in a group known as the LD Class – LD for Late Developers. This unfortunate tag resulted in a parent-backed campaign to get the class renamed. I interviewed just four people from the group and all felt there was a stigma to their class. They took their O–level GCE exams with the age-group below ours and made most of their friends within that year, few finding relationships with members of their own age in our year.

Twenty-five interviewees stayed on to the sixth form right through from the first year. Another five joined County High in the lower sixth straight from local secondary modern schools where they had obtained good O–level passes. Every one of the twenty-five spoke of the amazing change of atmosphere that descended on the school the moment they entered to start their sixth form. 'Suddenly', said one, 'we were adults.' There appears to have been an upsurge of good relations between staff and sixth formers. 'The biology teacher was a bit like an elder sister,' said a boy. 'She took our little group on trips and we all got very close.' Others reported that smiles wreathed faces once noted for scowls. A–level results at the end of those two years were very good, according to the headmaster.

The only major dispute during those terms involved about four boys who let their hair grow. When asked to get it cut they refused and all were barred from becoming prefects in their last year. Two said they still felt upset by the pettiness of that decision – but, in fairness, prefectships did not mean a great deal within the school, though reports to universities always included such information. There were many who stayed on to the sixth form who wondered why the first five years could not have been as relaxed as the last two. Only one boy thought the original discipline was better.

There was supposed to be a system of careers advice for pupils

26

about to leave the school, and one master took on extra responsibility for dealing with queries from pupils on careers. It was a derisory gesture. The personal talks for school-leavers were stereotyped to such an extent that gossip after the meetings showed how the official would give the same advice to scores of people with different abilities and personalities. 'He told me I ought to try a bank,' a girl would say. 'He said the same to me,' a colleague echoed. 'Really,' says a third, 'he told that to me too.'

The so-called careers master was nothing more than the teacher with a store cupboard large enough to keep the reams of literature from industry. This unsatisfactory hypocrisy was a sop to the school authorities, a manoeuvre to outwit parents and allay their worries. It was possibly a pupil's first glimpse of the impersonal world outside school. Few questions engendered as much criticism as that on careers advice.

Dagenham is an area where sport, particularly football, thrives. So it is no surprise that County High treated its soccer seriously. There were teams for every age-group and the whole culture of the school was centred on the three football pitches. The school heroes were free-scoring centre-forwards; boys spent every available minute of their breaks playing football on the asphalt with a ragged tennis ball; girls stood in drizzle on the touchline to cheer on the team. (Strange how boys never gave a second glance to the girls' hockey matches.) Many a boy dogged by constant academic disaster could walk with pride past the sports noticeboard or attend Monday morning assembly to hear his name mentioned in connection with the latest football victory. Boys did not play to escape lessons either, for, with the odd exception, matches were played on Saturday mornings, and it was rare for the eleven not to turn up. Those Saturdays were very much part of the culture, producing a knock-about camaraderie among the regular team members, in which zany behaviour became the norm. A whole range of meaningless banter and half-told jokes were built up, the keywords of which would convulse the team, the 'in crowd', and baffle outsiders. For a short time shoplifting became popular at away matches – dressing rooms would overflow with chocolate bars while semi-hysterical accounts were given of the thefts. Finally, one boy was caught and although the shopkeeper did not call the police or report the incident the theft habit stopped. This zaniness, combined with the local importance of soccer, made the footballers popular among the girls. But it made them less than popular with their contemporaries as I discovered on my survey.

The sport orientation at County High turned a lot of pupils –

boys and girls – against sport. One girl, generally regarded as one of the least rebellious in the year, took the risk of punishment to miss games lessons by hiding. A number of boys wrote each other false notes from home claiming continuous colds, unending backaches and recurring sprains . . . all in an attempt to sit out physical education. In the summer, weekly visits to the open air swimming pool (average temperature 66 deg. F) were too much for some who missed the coach with amazing regularity. Although I found a number of girls who disliked hockey, netball, rounders and athletics, it was among the boys I discovered a deep and lasting hatred for games. It was linked closely to their belief that being good at sport won favours from girls. Looking back over his school life, the first comment by one boy was: 'I only wish I could have played football better.'

Another said: 'There were those boys who played in the team and who played together in the top matches in games lessons. And then there were the twits, the idiots, like me. I played in some silly group where we hardly knew how to kick a ball. We didn't want to play but we had to. I hated everyone who liked football, especially as the girls always liked them.'

Cricket in the summer months did not produce the same kind of distinction among players or emotion among non-players. There were tennis courts, used more by girls than boys, but tennis was not popular. Summer in Dagenham was a temporary lull in the footballing frenzy.

Inter-school sports competition was organised on a House basis. Everyone entering the school was placed into one of the four Houses – Jenkins, Valence, Parsloes and Alibon – each named after ancient Dagenham manors. Apart from sporting contests, music and drama festivals were held on alternate years. These were promoted by enthusiastic teachers from each department and the former stemmed from the school choir, which was generally considered to be of high quality for its type, and which built up a fine repertoire. Members of the choir also had the distinction of sitting in the balcony at the back of the hall during morning assembly.

One of the more farcical events of the week was choir practice. Such was the fervour for football that a number of choir members would rather play during their lunchbreak than attend practice. This often resulted in the absence of the entire tenor section and robbed the girl sopranos of their essential treble lead. The music master would then send emissaries to discover the footballing choir boys and threaten them with imminent doom if they did not turn up immediately. Once coaxed, the sporting singers would shuffle in single file into the hall – hair askew, shirts hanging out, knees grubby and beaded with sweat – to be greeted by a neurotic tirade from the music master. Despite this it was an accomplished choir.

Ironically, little drama of this nature went on backstage in the school's annual plays which were expertly produced and well received. Apart from the previously mentioned *Antigone,* I recall Shaw's *Pygmalion,* Anouilh's *The Lark,* and N. F. Simpson's *One-Way Pendulum.* All had their merits.

There were also two debating societies, one for the junior section of the school, and one for the seniors. Neither was well organised and debates tended to be infrequent though fairly well attended. I remember taking part in one which debated whether money spent on advertising was wasted. It was a typical example and was not of a high standard.

There was a Service branch attached to the school – the Air Training Corps. Boys donned charcoal grey and marched around the school playground like badly-rehearsed toy soldiers. Camps were held; lectures on the use of firearms were given; books on flying were studied. But the uniformed squadron was not popular and numbers were small.

One other weekly after-school activity that drew its nucleus of regular supporters, and a few more besides, was the Friday detention. This was the one-hour official detention for those handed special 'detention slips', known as 'dets', for one or a series of misdemeanours committed during the week. Naughty boys and girls were required to sit quietly and write essays on subjects like 'The need for discipline in society' and 'Why I am here', or to inscribe 500 lines on a theme familiar to all schoolboys since the time of Bunter and Stalky & Co and before. The detention slips had to be signed by a parent and co-signed by the headmaster. Both meetings could be sticky for the boy or girl infrequently in trouble. But for those who were used to the process the regularity reduced the tension and made a nonsense of the deterrent. Detention was at the centre of some parent-school conflicts over discipline. 'It smacked of the Army,' said one father. A second said he thought detention showed that teachers were unable to control the class. And a third considered it petty. All three said they had complained at least once about detention and the bad effect they claimed it had on their children.

Caning was also carried out in what the headmaster considered to be serious breaches of discipline. He referred to it as his last resort. No pupil who was caned, and there were fifteen in the survey who admitted to it, complained.[4] Most said it hurt and a couple were embarrassed by the memory. One boy said: 'It was bending over that hurt me more than the actual caning. It was horrible sticking your bum up in the air. It was undignified.'

It has not been my aim in this look at school life to give more than a glimpse of what the pupils thought of County High and of their education. Their attitudes will be studied much more closely in the following chapters. It is vital, however, to consider their opinions in the light of the facts. County High was a 'second division' grammar school situated in a working class area with a predominantly working class intake of pupils. The staff, which included many graduates, was almost wholly middle class.[5] The views of parents and teachers were as different as their life-styles. The school's range of education was limited, its main aim being to coach pupils for the passing of a maximum of eight GCE O–levels. Discussion lessons were rare. There was a great emphasis on sporting attainments. The premises, though tight on space, were adequate and certainly better than nearly all the rest of Dagenham's schools. The boys and girls who chose to stay on into the sixth form years for an A–level course discovered that the atmosphere of the earlier years was not a Law of Nature after all. Schools could be pleasant.

PART TWO

The Interviews

Middle Class Perpetuation

The working class ghetto that was Dagenham was bordered by the reserves of the middle class – Ilford to the north, and Romford, Hornchurch and Upminster to the east. Here were the quiet, tree-lined avenues of semi-detached desirable residences with bay windows and climbing roses over porches decorated with electrified coaching lanterns and warnings to hawkers and circulars. Miniature trees encircled billiard table lawns and stone bird baths; double wrought iron gates led up to spacious garages; and solid, wooden doors opened on to rich, carpeted hallways with wide stairways. These were the sturdily built houses of the mid-war monied middle classes. Unlike modern houses, planned to use up every inch with tiny gardens, these were notable for having plenty of space within and without. Gardens were expansive enough for cricket pitch length lawns running down to sheds, usually concealed behind a trellis of honeysuckle, and beyond lay the vegetable patch. The multi-coloured flower beds were reflected inside by chintz-covered three-piece suites offset by dark, polished cabinets and tables and sombre drapes. There was an atmosphere of permanence about these homes, a feeling that this heavy furniture in a big brick house mirrored the established order of things. They, the houses and their occupants, were here to stay.

Surrounding these secluded, comfortable avenues were estates of smaller private houses, sometimes a bungaloid enclave, often a group of mock Tudor terraces and semis. The epitome of such an area was Upminster, where four of the sample lived; another was neighbouring Hornchurch, home of two. Ilford and Romford were a little different in style due to their shopping centres. This created a bustling residential area where many big houses were converted into flats, making for some mixed housing and a mixture of classes near the centres. Nevertheless, clearly defined middle class retreats were apparent. Three of the sample were drawn from Ilford, and one came from Rush Green, an area of small private houses on the border of Romford and Dagenham.

There are, of course, as many subjective divisions in the middle class as in the working class, and this sample of ten included people from differing groups. The one link between all was that they belonged to the middle class who used State secondary schools rather than private ones. Mr Frost, Mr Green, Mr Parry and Mr Moore ran their own businesses; Mr Barton was a senior local government officer; Mr Carter was a banker; Mr Linton, an accountant; and Mr Denning, a banquetting director. The other two, Mr Millett and Mr Andrews, both worked for Ford's, but not in the traditional middle class executive capacity. Mr Millett was a supervisor, a job to which many working class men aspired, but his background was the determining class factor. His father was a senior civil servant, and Mr Millett was privately educated, by tutor, at home. Mr Andrews' job was still less middle class in character, being a quality control inspector, but the family's class was set by inherent wealth and, unusually, by the wife. Mrs Andrews was a senior school teacher. Certainly, their house was in the most settled middle class area and it was one of the biggest I visited in the course of my study.

It may be considered surprising that the middle class, so much more informed and aware of the differing educational opportunities, and concerned about class differences between areas, should have chosen County High in Dagenham for their children. [1] I could not discover the reasons in all ten cases, but undeniably two major factors played a part: the 'bulge year' and the borderline pass system. Dagenham's second division status determined intake, and three of the group, it would appear, got borderline passes at 11-plus. They, and three others, found themselves placed in their fourth choice grammar school – 'the one my parents and I thought I'd never get,' said one boy. Most of the middle class sample were surprised at the decision but only one protested. Angela Moore said: 'We put down Dagenham as fourth choice but my father was so shocked he wrote to the education office about it. He couldn't make them change the decision.'

Mr Carter mentioned the matter within the family. Susan Carter recalled: 'My father was against me going to Dagenham but I don't think he did anything about it.' Roger Parry went simply because his sister who had gone before him had enjoyed life at the school, but this personal knowledge was unique. For the other six who entered aged eleven the school was something of a mystery.

Two of the sample went to the school after passing the 13-plus, and at this age entrants had no choice but to accept the local authority's decision. Alistair Linton said: 'Dagenham was chosen

34

for me. My father had no say either.' One joined after succeeding at 16 in the GCE O–level exams at a secondary modern school. Again, it was a case of going to the school that was nominated.

For five who started in the first form in 1958 it was like discovering a new world . . . a school they had never seen, in an area they had never visited, populated in the main by children from a different class. In the passing of time their initial reactions have been forgotten but they all recalled feeling different. First, there was Dagenham and the Becontree Estate to contend with.

Angela Moore said she and her parents had to consult a map to discover where the school was. 'I felt I needed that map every day at first. I couldn't believe streets could look so much alike.'

Susan Carter said: 'I didn't know what a council house was until I went to Dagenham. I think I felt a lot of sympathy for the people who came from there. After all, it wasn't a very nice place, was it? And I knew I was different – I didn't have six sisters and a gran living with me for a start.'

Michael Barton's original impression was that the district 'was on the rough side'. At that time he did little to test his theory. 'I travelled through it on the bus to and from school,' he said, 'and so I didn't see much. I never went for walks round it or anything like that. I didn't make friends with anyone who lived in Dagenham.'

This was true also for Dennis Green and John Andrews, who found friendship together travelling from Upminster but did not mix socially with their new colleagues. Dennis said: 'I was always glad to get out of Dagenham in the early days.' Back home they tended to continue friendships with their primary school and church friends. All five recalled a certain shyness in the face of other boys and girls in their classes. A notable distinction between them and their new classmates was speech. John said: 'The fact that I spoke better grammar made me class conscious from the day I arrived.' Susan Carter agreed: 'I knew I had a better upbringing because their speech was worse than mine. My mother became worried after a while because she thought my speech was affected.'

It was not always the case of *how* things were said but *what* was said. Susan told how her interest in sport drew her into friendship within Dagenham quite early in her school life. She said: 'I sometimes found it difficult to understand the other girls. One half-term holiday I went to see a couple of the netball team at Dagenham. When I got to the house one girl said: "Let's play on the council." I just didn't know what she meant.' [2]

The three boys did not find sporting links. None were particularly proficient at football and, aware of the school's soccer

35

bias, they made great efforts to show willing at the game. John Andrews said he always wished he could have played football better, and thought himself physically inferior to the other boys. Michael Barton said: 'I was always getting knocked about at soccer. I just wasn't as tough as the rest, but I pretended to be.' He made up for his inability on the football field by doing well at cricket and table tennis. John Andrews represented the school at athletics. Dennis Green did not concern himself at all with sport.

Brian Frost lived in a Dagenham border area and had gone to a primary school within the borough. His adjustment in terms of class had been made from his earliest schooldays and it was much later in life before he said he discovered a 'difference'. Naturally, he was aware that he lived in a bigger house and that he 'did not live on that awful Estate'.

He said he got on well with his classmates at school but was extremely condescending towards them in our talk. 'Dagenham people,' he said, 'were a good type, but quite honestly a bit thick. I felt well adjusted at school but somehow superior because my family were better off. I suppose I was a snob then though I didn't let on. I'm even more of a snob now.'

He said he had enjoyed his schooldays and his social life in Dagenham 'but now I never admit I come from there. It has a bad ring to it.' (In contrast to this, and an illustration of the stratification within the middle class itself, is Susan Carter's view. 'I'm glad I went to Dagenham,' she concluded, 'because it stopped me being a snob.') Brian had a lot to say for himself in the classroom and was aware of his verbosity. He commented: 'I always said what I thought even though I knew others thought I was just being pompous. I suppose I had too much self-confidence.'

Roger Parry knew what to expect at County High from his elder sister. He had seen her doing her homework and understood therefore the kind of attitude needed to succeed. He was not extrovert by nature but he built up a reputation, in spite of his shyness, for being able to answer almost every question asked of a class. 'I became known as the class know-all,' he said. 'It came to be expected by the other children and the teachers that I would know the answer to just about anything. It made me very worried that I'd answer wrong some time.'

Alistair Linton passed his 13-plus at Gaynes Secondary Modern

School in Upminster. Although he was immediately struck by what he called 'a lack of discipline' at County High he was untroubled by the change. The reason was that the headmaster lived just down the road from him, and the senior history master was his Sunday School teacher. 'Naturally enough,' he remarked, 'that had an effect on the way I behaved.' Dagenham he thought was dirty – 'so different from Upminster' – and he disliked it.

Jean Denning arrived at the same time having passed her late entrance examination while at private school in Ilford. The first difference she noted was speech. She was not enamoured either with Dagenham.

For David Millett entry to County High was delayed until after he passed seven GCE O–levels at Mayfield Secondary Modern School in Ilford. Dagenham was, for him, the image of dull socialism. Of the school, he said he felt at first out of depth. The transformation from the high-pressure teaching at Mayfield to the relaxed atmosphere of a grammar school sixth form took him by surprise. He was also upset by the other pupils having a knowledge of languages, and said he was aware that he was not liked when he arrived. However, he added: 'I could not feel inferior to the rest.'

Home lives for all ten were stable and none could recollect their parents having any special financial worries. I deduced from our conversation that in every case the father played the dominant role in the house, making all policy decisions. All went on regular holidays and some went abroad in an era when package holidays were much less popular, and more expensive, than they are today. Their social activities included membership of Scout and Guide groups, tennis clubs and church organisations. Church-going was a regular habit for seven.

There were few clashes with parental authority. Susan Carter suffered from an over-strict father with whom she found communication difficult but this was compensated, she believed, by her mother's influence. She was scared to take home her annual report, for example, because her father's criticisms made her feel inferior. This resulted in her being timid in the classroom, too. 'I hated being asked questions. They put me in a state of shock.' She added: 'I honoured my parents and teachers always. I had a great respect for other people's wishes and I would never go against society for the sake of it.' The stress at home 'gave me nightmares about French, and I hated English lessons.'

Roger Parry strove for more independence at home and became moody with his parents at times when he thought he was not getting enough freedom. However, this appeared not to have been a

37

deep conflict. He got a lot of encouragement at home.

Jean Denning's mother died when she was four, leaving her upbringing to her grandmother and father. It was, she considered, an easy-going relationship which put little pressure on her academically. John Andrews and Michael Barton were fortunate to have teachers in the house. Their mothers both taught and offered advice from a professional viewpoint. In John's case – his mother being a senior school teacher – it was an invaluable help. David Millett said his home background was 'success-orientated', and Brian Frost reported that his parents were tremendously interested in his schooling.

Alistair Linton and Dennis Green spoke of parental encouragement; of careful advice; of considered attitudes. Nearly all parents in this sample pushed their children in a direction they seemed to want to take.

The home environment offered a lot of security and, except for Brian Frost, none were drawn at weekends or during the evenings to Dagenham. Susan Carter said: 'My father would never have allowed me to go there at night even if I'd wanted to, which I didn't.'

Social pursuits at home were not augmented by a desire to join in at school. Four were at various times in the choir; three took an active part in debating; and eight got involved in various sports activities. But the impression I gained was one of apathy towards after-school enterprises, although Angela Moore's main memory of school centred on the hockey field. Roger Parry tried in his last year to start a film society, but without success.

Although initial relations with their new classmates were strained, it was natural that pupils in this group should find the middle class staff to their liking. Parry had a stronger than normal link at this level because his parents took a French assistant teacher into their household during her year-long stay at County High. He recalled conversations at dinner, on philosophy and religion for instance, that must have been of benefit to his education and which were undoubtedly not open to working class pupils.

Friendships were made over a period of time. Parry was a member of a close-knit clique of four. An academic group, the quartet were all in the A stream, all stayed into the sixth form and all went on to university. 'I was closer to those three than I've been to anyone, excluding my wife, since I left school,' said Parry. Those were carefully chosen words, signifying the depth of that tight relationship. The four chose different paths after school and are not now in contact.[3]

Jean Denning spoke of a similar clique of six girls within her LD class, but it appeared to be more fluid and fragile than Parry's group. She has, though, maintained a slight contact with one old schoolfriend. John Andrews and Dennis Green, despite being in different streams, B and C respectively, maintained a friendship throughout their school careers, only branching out into wider circles in their sixth form years. Green still keeps in touch with a couple of friends made at that stage. Michael Barton, Alistair Linton, Susan Carter and Angela Moore all had wider circles of friends, mainly through sports interests which cut across the streaming divisions. Linton is the only one of the three to continue an old school friendship. With an almost clinical detachment, Susan Carter remarked: 'I cut all my friends when I left.'

Brian Frost's circle was the widest of all ten. His extrovert personality and commitment to diverse activities – football, choir, piano lessons, debating – led him to make a number of friends. He was also the only one of this sample to clash continually with school authority. Brian was well placed in the B stream and admitted to having 'a tremendous ego'. He said: 'I felt superior to almost everyone. I always wanted to excel and I loved praise. I fed on it. I cheated in an examination and came top. I loved the feeling so much I couldn't stop cheating. I finally got caught but although I hated my father being told I never stopped doing it. I loved to succeed.' He also got involved in pranks, was impertinent and had a reputation for bullying. 'I once got caned after a fight when I refused to apologise to my opponent.' He was the classic example of the choir boy with an innocent face who behind the scenes created havoc. When asked about discipline at school he replied: 'If there'd been harsher discipline it would have been even more fun defeating it.' That remark perfectly sums up his schoolboy attitude.

None of the others got into any sort of trouble though Michael Barton said he was accused of 'dumb insolence' on one report – a remark he felt was not unjustified. He objected to school discipline, and made his hostility plain, in direct contrast to the others who felt the discipline was fair and that there was a minimal imposition of rules. One or two thought it, if anything, lax. It was, according to Linton and Green, a matter for individual teachers – some were stricter than others, but none was too severe.

Seven of the group were in no doubt that they did not get a good education at County High and were highly critical of their schooling. Michael Barton was in the C stream. He said: 'My results speak for themselves. I left County High after five years with one O–level. I joined the sixth form at Abbs Cross [4] and a year

39

later I'd got five more passes. Dagenham was a waste of time.'
Roger Parry, from the A stream, said: 'The whole emphasis of our
education was wrong. The school was geared only to providing
university entrance.[5] We should have had a much more general
education in our early years.' He also thought the standard of
teaching was poor. Susan Carter, who left after the fifth form with
four O–levels, thought it a 'pretty hopeless school'. She was in the
B stream but believed she could have done as well by going to the
local secondary modern in Upminster.

Jean Denning, in the LD class, said: 'The teachers were not
really up to the job.' And her LD classmate, Alistair Linton,
considered it an unexceptional education. 'I've got where I've got
by my education since leaving,' he said.

David Millett, the sixth form entrant, was the only one able to
give a truly comparative opinion. He said: 'I knew before I went to
Dagenham County High that it wasn't a leading academic centre.
There wasn't enough stimulation by the staff.'

One or two were critical of various members of staff and of the
lack of opportunity to broaden their education. However, it was
difficult to get precise criticisms – an appraisal of the curriculum,
the merits of the teaching methods, the possible alternatives. Only
Roger Parry was prepared to suggest possble improvements to the
system. His ideas are interesting: geography should have dealt
more with social anthropology; history should have related to
up-to-date institutions; science should have been more down to
earth, teaching about fuses, lights and cars; mathematics lessons,
too, should have been allied to everyday practicalities. All this,
thought Roger, would have made the syllabus more enlivening in
the first three years, gaining the real interest of pupils before two
examination training years. He thought exams 'tended to be the
best method of assessment,' and added: 'Discussions generally
make for bad lessons.'

There was support on this point from Michael Barton and Susan
Carter, who said: 'Current affairs discussion is not worth having
with schoolchildren. It only affects people when they're earning and
owning.' John Andrews, too, was sceptical about current affairs
periods – 'It's idealistic to think everyone wants to know' – but he
was not against the idea in principle. The others favoured open
discussions in classroom on current topics but all recalled that
attempts to introduce them in the fifth form at County High were
not successful.

These lessons, known as 'civics', were generally considered at the
time as worthless, excuses for pranks and wisecracking. However,

they were never taken very seriously by the teachers designated to lead them, and it was only junior staff who were given the responsibility. The ideal of imbuing a class of fifteen-year-olds with the ways of the world was bedevilled by embarrassment on the pupils' side and the inexperience of teachers.

Alistair Linton remembered enjoying current affairs lessons at his secondary modern school but was disenchanted with County High's attempts. Jean Denning said simply: 'They were useless.' This lack of adequate classroom discussion lay behind the poor standard of debating and is, perhaps, the direct reason for the low number of articulate ex-pupils. [6]

Few lessons allowed for free discussion, and one that many might have thought would, was religious knowledge. But it was a purely factual study, dealing with Old Testament history, and even the headmaster was given to criticise its narrowness in his retrospective look at school life. With seven churchgoers in this sample I expected some support for the teaching of religious knowledge. However, most thought it an unnecessary subject and Michael Barton, one of those who still regularly attends church, said: 'Authority and humility don't mix. Religious teaching turns away rather than encourages.' There was little obvious propaganda in the lessons though a case may easily be made out against the teaching of Christianity in isolation. One of the main points to emerge was that the teaching of comparative religions would have been of far more value, and this would also have inevitably led to discussions. Taking it a stage further, Angela Moore thought that correctly taught lessons on religion would have 'opened up to include the fields of philosophy and sociology. Ours did not.'

Nine of the sample studied French – for at least five years – but only Angela Moore said she could speak the language now. Jean Denning said she regularly wrote to, and occasionally conversed with, a French penfriend but was far from fluent. Two others said they could understand French if it was spoken slowly and had a smattering of the language themselves. The consensus of opinion was that passing a written examination was far removed from everyday speech. The thirst for linguistic knowledge had been soured for many by the hours spent pondering over the application of an irregular verb in its pluperfect form. The French oral test at GCE O–level was a sideline to the written examination. One or two thought the reverse should have been true. It is further evidence of the written word taking precedence in the classroom over the spoken word.

Five of the group left school at the end of their fifth year – aged

41

16. Michael Barton simply changed schools. Susan Carter took a secretarial course at Hornchurch College of Further Education. 'I lost out not having shorthand-typing lessons at County High,' she said. She was good at sports and her earlier ambition had been to teach games but she needed O–level English and that was not among her four passes. Ironically, she passed it while at college but was already set on her career.

Jean Denning left with two O–levels, and after a couple of months as a chambermaid in a seaside hotel, a working holiday, she said her father booked her into a secretarial college. A strange decision since her aim had been to become a cookery demonstrator. Brian Frost got the required five O–levels for entering the sixth form, and was in two minds as to whether he should stay on, but he decided to gain his independence and took a job. Angela Moore said her parents were much older than those of her friends, and her father 'had a traditional attitude towards girls'. He wanted her to marry and refused to allow her to stay on to the sixth form in spite of her eight O–levels. Instead she took a course in retail display at a technical college.

Alistair Linton stayed on for an extra year with the specific object of passing the O-levels he had failed. Alistair left with five and then took a job.

The other four – including David Millett from secondary modern – became sixth form students. John Andrews studied biological sciences and left with seven O–levels and two A–levels, going on to Leeds University. Roger Parry concentrated on physics and mathematics, leaving with nine O–levels and three A–levels. It was the culmination of a remarkable academic school career in which he had finished top of the A stream on all but one occasion. In his last year he was the deputy head boy. He went to Sussex University. Dennis Green did badly in his original O–level examinations and stayed on an extra year in the fifth form to get the necessary five for sixth form study. He then spent two years in the sixth, gaining one A–level, and left aged 19 to go on to college.

David Millett's examination results after his lower sixth year were disappointing. 'I suppose I needed the pressure of Mayfield again,' he said. He pressured himself instead over the following months and the effort was rewarded by three A–levels. His passes were not good enough for the university place he wanted, so in a year spent working in a factory and an office, he re-sat his economic history exam and obtained a higher grade. He then won a place at Lancaster University.

As for careers advice, all ten reported its existence but none thought it was worthwhile. The disorganisation of the scheme was summed up by Dennis Green: 'I always seemed to be elsewhere whenever the careers officer turned up.' It was not an isolated cry. Jean Denning said an administration error robbed her of advice. John Andrews was sent on an agricultural college course, but only because he wanted to be a farmer and requested it, and he said he was unimpressed by the scheme since the officer showed a lack of enthusiasm for the venture. Of the others, some had no advice and some had a little. Nobody was influenced by their careers guidance at school.

By the time I came to do my survey seven of the ten were married; one was on the verge of doing so; and another was interested in following suit, having just had a broken engagement. Only two had children, and a third said his wife was expecting. Of the seven men, six had pursued careers which, in the main, had followed logical courses up the scale in position and responsibility and, of course, in salary. One of the girls who remained single had done the same and the other two girls had married men following a similar pattern. The exception was David Millett who was just finishing a post-graduate course at Sheffield University. He rented a cottage in South Yorkshire in contrast to the other six married people who were buying their homes. Both the unmarried men lived with their parents in Upminster, but the one about to marry was in the process of purchasing a house further into Essex. Jean Denning still lived in Ilford, not far from the place where she was brought up, but the others had moved away from their childhood homes. Two lived in Essex; one had gone to Orpington in Kent; one to Dorset; one to Solihull, Warwickshire, and the other to South London.

Three lived in new houses, the kind that have sprung up in little estates on the edge of villages and towns all over Britain since the early 1960s. The exteriors are plain with big windows framing the main living areas. Lounges-cum-dining-rooms are approximately the same size as the gardens. Inside – a range of accessories from central heating to wall sockets for electric shavers. The taste in furniture was conservative, traditional, polished softwood contrasting with more modern three-piece suites offset by pastel shades for carpets, curtains and walls. The main difference from their childhood homes was the absence of bric-a-brac. The coffee table might sport one silver cigarette lighter, the television a vase. But there was little clutter. Bookshelves were rare ... books rarer still. The same was true for the three living in older houses. Two had carried out extensive conversions to make the interiors indistinguishable from their modern counterparts, and the third was contemplating doing the same. One item of furniture all seven possessed was a television, but none had a colour set. A couple had stereo record players. Only one of the sample was without a car and he was hoping to buy one soon. Jean Denning and her husband shared two cars. There was, in all but the case of Millett, an air of prosperity about their homes and a complacency in their attitudes. The six male wage earners had an average income of more than £2,600 a year.

John Andrews was unmarried and lived at his parents' house 'because I love the comforts'. He got a B.Sc. (Agriculture) and took a job as adviser in the research department of a farm machinery manufacturers. His farming ambitions thwarted by the realisation of the immense cost involved, he said he had maintained his contact with farming 'by the back door'. He hoped in time to be promoted to the position of export demonstrator, a role which would involve world travel. He had been engaged but the relationship broke up after a year. He said he had several girlfriends and a good social life, part of which was spent helping out at the local Scout group. Having gone to university in Leeds his friends were widely spread but he maintained contact with several circles. He was not, however, in touch with anyone from County High.

Roger Parry also got a B.Sc., but was uncertain quite what to do when he left university. He took a couple of casual jobs for six months while he made up his mind and then landed a post in the Midlands as a research scientist with a car accessories firm. He had been there for four years when we met. He was frustrated by the job and hoped to branch out into a different sphere like management. He met his wife, who worked in an office, because she had been a neighbour when he first moved to Solihull.

Dennis Green had wanted to be an architect but ended up doing a college course in chartered surveying. He emerged with a diploma and got a job with the Civil Service. He was happy with his occupation and wished to make a success of it. He met his wife, a secretary, at his tennis club. Now they spend much of their social life at a local hockey and tennis club. A strange twist this. Dennis took no active part in the rough and tumble of school sports but later turned to the more middle class pursuits on offer outside.

Michael Barton's valuable year at another secondary school enabled him to go to college. He studied for a public health diploma and on winning it took various appointments with London boroughs as a public health officer. When we met he was working for Barking Council from its Dagenham headquarters. It had given him an acute insight into an area which at school he had avoided. After some consideration he said the district 'lacked charm'! He expected promotion in his job but had no definite career ambitions. He met his wife while playing badminton. They had a child which, they said, restricted their social life although Michael continued to play badminton and golf. He was also a regular churchgoer.

Alistair Linton was two months away from marriage to a girl he met at his tennis club. He still played football. His fiancée had also revived his former church-going habits. He never stopped studying after leaving school and joined the electricity board as an accounts trainee. After seven years of promotion and examination passes he left to become a management accountant with an air transport firm. He was also on his way to a degree in business studies. His father was an accountant and it had been his schoolboy ambition to achieve the same.

Angela Moore's father was determined that his daughter should marry on leaving school. Ten years later she is equally determined to remain single. 'I'm avoiding marriage at the moment because I'm worried that I may be bored. People make me bored.' Angela concentrated instead on work, although the changes in job are another pointer to her philosophy of refusing to be bored. After a year at college she became a fashion store display supervisor – a euphemism for a window dresser – and 18 months later took a job as a buyer with a nationwide clothing store. In the following five years she had two similar jobs, though with growing responsibility. When we met she was making inroads into the advertising business as a junior executive. She said: 'I've got no long term ambitions, except that I suppose I'll get married in time. I'd like to hope I choose someone who has his own company. I'm sick of a salary – I want a share in the profits.' Angela's salary had enabled her to buy a bungalow in Kent – in which her parents lived – while she stayed during the week in a London flat.

Brian Frost's first steps up the ladder of security were unsteady. He tried a shipping firm and a couple of insurance companies before settling for a foreign bank. He had been there for nearly seven years and was assistant to the chief clerk. His extrovert nature was evident again: 'I have no difficulty getting on with people. They like me there. I run the firm's football team and the office medical aid scheme.'

He also played squash and continued his interest in music, regretting perhaps that he passed up chances to further his musical education. 'I suppose,' he said with no hint of humour, 'I could have been a second Dudley Moore.' [7] He retained also his strong

45

links with the church. He had been head chorister at St Georges Church in Dagenham as a boy and now went regularly to his new local church. 'It showed my strength of character that I kept going when others fell by the wayside,' he said. 'I was so proud of going to church that I did tend to come the big Christian.' His main aims were wealth and happiness.

Jean Denning had various secretarial jobs through the years until she had a child. Her son was two when we met and she was expecting another child. She was introduced to her husband, a building contractor, by a friend. She was looking forward to moving away from Ilford and to raising her children. She did not anticipate returning to work until they had grown up. She enjoyed cooking, she said, for house parties.

After training at college Susan Carter spent three years as a secretary at a London firm. Then she went on holiday to Dorset, fell in love with the place and stayed. She did a short spell of hotel work before joining a bank as a secretary. She met her husband at a folk club. Her ambition was to have children and see her husband succeed at his job as a draughtsman.

While others were earning and learning, David Millett was simply learning. After graduating from Lancaster with a degree in economics he moved across to Sheffield to do post graduate studies in economic history. He was about to get his M.A. when we met. During his final year he had earned a little money as a part-time tutor. He hoped to win a permanent lectureship post but was uncertain where he would end up. At Lancaster, he met his wife, a girl from a working class background in Bootle. She had a regular wage packet as an English teacher at a comprehensive school. David said: 'I'm fortunate in having a fairly intellectual wife to share my reading habits.' Their social life was centred on the university and its diverse activities, and they also went to the cinema and theatre.

These are the stories of well co-ordinated attempts to attain financial security using, if necessary, the available facilities of further education – university, college, night class, postal course. They may not have had interrupted educational beginnings like their parents, or been on such unsteady a financial footing, but they had settled far earlier into acceptance of their lot. Their passive acquiescence of the status quo is well reflected in their political outlook. Six said they had voted Conservative and would continue so to do; two said they were hedging towards the Liberal Party as the soft alternative to the Tories; and one, Roger Parry, would vote Labour. He said his ideal of the perfect Labour politician was Roy

Jenkins. Only David Millett had swung away from the Conservative upbringing that led him to be a young Tory. He said: 'I'm generally Left wing. If I vote I give it to the most Left wing candidate available. However, I regard myself as a liberal not a revolutionary. I fit the *New Statesman-Guardian* image of a Left winger.'

Michael Barton was the only union member among the ten, belonging to the National and Local Government Officers Association. He was in favour of the Industrial Relations Act. All the Tories said they felt the unions had gone too far. A Labour supporter also backed the Act. There was an air of tolerance to the question of immigration though Susan Carter and Alistair Linton gave unswerving support to the view that Britain should close its door to black people. Their Press was conservative in tone. Of the seven who read a newspaper every day, three took *The Times,* three the *Daily Telegraph,* and one the *Daily Express.* Few read any magazine except for occupational reasons and only a couple read books. Library tickets largely went unused. Current affairs on television appeared to be the concern of only two people, and all were selective in their viewing habits.

Maybe all have some of the traits that have made the middle classes appear pre-eminent in our society — self-reliance, common sense, thrift and diligence. Different though their schoolday home lives were from their working class contemporaries, it is more than a little significant to see how alike in attitudes and lifestyles they are now as adults.

Divided We Learn

The 112 working class boys and girls of County High who became the men and women of this study were of varied character and appearance — some were shy and a few of us were extrovert; some wary while others were anxious to please; some were sure of themselves and others, I felt, were emotionally unstable. The one linking factor for all was our working class background. Its effect on our lives was different in scores of small ways that I hope to illustrate in the coming pages. But there can be no shadow of doubt that the working class environment had a positive effect. It was more marked than many of us would admit to or realised. In the case of most people this is a story of flight . . . from their class and from their past. For some, it is a record of frustration and unhappiness. For a few, the story of acceptance or complacency, apathy or ignorance.

Sixty-three of the group lived in the Borough of Dagenham. Of these, 48 lived in council houses — 31 of which were on the Becontree Estate — and five lived in rented accommodation. The other ten were privately housed. It means that 49 of the pupils travelled into Dagenham. Twenty-one of these lived in council estates in Barking, South Ockendon and Elm Park. Four more rented their homes and 24 lived in private houses, including ten who came from Hornchurch. One hundred and six of us started at County High in the first form, two more joined after passing the 13-plus and the other four arrived in the sixth form to study GCE A–levels.

In tracing these people I spoke to many of their parents, most of whom were warm and helpful. I would be invited in while mothers rummaged for wedding pictures and school reports. I did, however, have a couple of amusing experiences. One father said sternly through a chain-locked door: 'Go away. My girl doesn't want that sort of publicity. Go on, push off.' A week later the daughter — traced through another contact — apologised for her father's behaviour. She said: 'He's a security man, you see, and it's affected

48

the way he thinks.'

Then there was the mother, who once I explained that I wished to meet her daughter again after having known her at school ten years before, looked most sympathetic and gushed: 'Ooh, you're too late. She's already married.'

Parents often revelled in the opportunity for nostalgic reflection and I sometimes spent as long with them as their children. The fathers' occupations give a clue to the kind of people they are, and the variety of backgrounds my contemporaries were drawn from. Among the private house dwellers were a few who had worked their way up to middle management, a couple at Ford's; one in local government; another in a hospital. Many had got their feet on to the rungs of lower management in factories, as supervisors and foremen and inspectors. And a number had 'made good money' in the lucrative Fleet Street printing industry. A few more worked in the East End docks. The council house tenants numbered foremen among their ranks too, but most had not taken any step towards management. Twenty-one of this sample – nearly one third of those living in council homes – worked at Ford's at the time of the survey or had recently retired from the plant.[1] Most of them worked on the assembly line or in the foundry. Apart from factory workers there were tradesmen: butchers, bakers and milkmen; those in the public services, postmen, railwaymen and policemen; and building workers, like painters, carpenters, joiners and plasterers. Most had steady jobs. Very few remembered fathers being out of work. Several had retired by the time of my survey, though half of them had taken light jobs soon after leaving.

About half the wives worked at some stage during the children's school lives, most of them in full-time employment. A few worked for Ford's canteen or in local light industry. Others were cleaners or shop assistants. A number did clerical work in small offices. The reason, in nearly every case, was to help the family budget. 'It's the difference between us having a holiday or not,' said one mother. No woman followed a career. If they did not work specifically for extra money they did so out of boredom. Said one, a canteen helper: 'Once the children went to school I couldn't find anything to do about the house. I never got on with the neighbours so I decided to go to work. It did the trick lovely. I met people and I was happy.'

Some parents had moved out of the area because they claimed it was unfriendly. Most had stayed because they said anywhere else would not be so friendly. It was a contradiction made all the more difficult to untangle by the claim that Dagenham represented the friendliness of the old East London communities from which most of its population had sprung. This is a view which may be sincerely held but very few of those who held it were of an age to have remembered the East End of which they talked. It appeared to be a phrase they trotted out on all occasions when similarly questioned. It's true that they may have made friends among their neighbours – but there were few outward signs in Dagenham of the kind of communal matiness displayed in the pre-war East End.[2] There has also been since the war a far greater tendency for women to work during the day, which was very different from the pre-war 'housewife' of Stepney and Poplar.

The Becontree Estate planners had tried hard to create communities by their arrangement of houses in squares and cul-de-sacs, but the ploy failed. People lived inside their homes – not outside on the streets. Houses in Dagenham, whether on the Becontree Estate or on the local council's estates, were not roomy. The larger versions had one downstairs room in which the family lived – the 'back room', a cosy place with a solid-looking settee set in front of an open fire. There was usually a television in the corner, a lamp standard in another, a table against one wall with wooden chairs around it. There was a clutter of personal memorabilia overflowing from mantelpiece, table and window sill. Old letters propped against china ornaments; pill bottles next to a clock that rarely gave the correct time; a little jar containing collar bones, hair clips and pencil stubs; a vase with plastic roses faded by the years and weighed down by dust; in a rack at the side of the fireplace a *TV Times* and copies of the past week's *Daily Mirror*. All this was in contrast to the impeccably tidy 'front room'. Here the arm chairs had antimacassars, the carpet was hardly worn, the ornaments were arrayed on a polished sideboard. 'I keep it nice for guests,' said one mother. I well remember being shown into one of these chilly front rooms at a friend's house so that we could talk away from the noise of television and younger brothers and sisters. The front room always seemed cold after the roaring fire next door.

Kitchens tended to be small and untidy but scrupulously clean. There was often a step down into the kitchen from the hallway, as if you were entering a special part of the house. In the smaller houses there was only one 'living room' on the ground level. This one room would be used for all activities – for meals and leisure, for the weekly ironing and a schoolchild's daily homework. There was little difference in the council houses elsewhere. Layouts were very much the same in South Ockendon or Barking, Elm Park or Tilbury.

The situation in privately owned houses was hardly different.

The majority of the children lived in homes organised in much the same way as those of their council house friends. The rooms in some were no bigger and parents had a similar lifestyle. One major difference between all working class homes and their middle class opposites was the absence of bookshelves. If there was a bookcase in a working class home it contained what might best be described as romantic fiction. Sometimes a twelve-volume set of encyclopaedias stood out at the end of a shelf – the result of high pressure selling 'for the good of your child' from a doorstep representative. Only one person in this sample lived in what could be called a large house, a multi-roomed detached residence. It was bought by a man who had risen to position of overseer in the print trade – but it was clearly a working class household. The same was true for all those who had moved into the middle class areas. The buying of a house represented the growing wealth of the working class and the parallel growth of independence from their class. For many, the purchasing of property became an ambition beyond which there was nothing further. They might be stuck in a job which was boring, which afforded little opportunity and from which there was no escape. But they were able to flee their environment instead. This upper working class, for want of a better description, formed about a third of the sample.

There were two people who did not fit into either the traditional working class category or this upper working class. For their backgrounds, while closer to those of the middle class than the working class, had followed working class lines. These were of the 'sunken middle class'.[3] One was the daughter of an Army Major who committed suicide soon after she was born, leaving her mother without enough money to continue their former life-style; and the second was the daughter of a university graduate, a trained pharmacist, who fled the house, again leaving the mother to cope financially. Both girls therefore had middle class grandparents on one side. They suffered some financial hardship in their single-parent homes, but noticeably less than the two council house boys in a similar situation. The girls also expressed their 'difference' from people around them in much the same way as the middle class children – and it showed. 'I was ridiculed as a snob,' said one.

Very few mothers or fathers stayed on at school beyond the age of 14.[4] There were two main reasons: the war and shortage of money. Further education was not one of the priorities for the teenage generation which emerged in the early 1940s – even if the child had desired it. And many said staying on at school would have cost the family too much. Earning meant more to the family as a unit than learning. 'My parents couldn't have afforded it though I always wished I had carried on,' said one Dagenham man in his early fifties. 'I was very quick at school. I picked up things and I did well. But you didn't get the encouragement in them days. Not like now. Everything's on a plate.' Children were made aware of their parents' educational frustration. 'My dad's very clever,' said one girl. 'He knows a lot more than me and he still reads a lot. If he'd had the opportunities I've had he would have been Prime Minister.' That particular claim was unique but the cry was common. Fathers I met as a schoolboy, and during the survey, were often dispirited men. Out of disgust they would sometimes refuse to even discuss their jobs. 'It's awful where I work,' said a Ford's foundryman. 'I hate it. I've worked there nearly 20 years and it's affected my life. My wife will tell you. I get moody in the week. I suffer with nerves.'

Another man, a factory production line worker, said: 'When I left the Navy there was no work around. I had two kids by then and I had to take the first thing that came along. I always meant to do better, to go somewhere else, but the chance never seemed to come up . . . well, I suppose it did. But by then I couldn't afford to take the risk.'

A third, a plasterer, conveyed the ideology of many who disliked their daily job. 'When I saw my boy growing up I said to my wife: "Right, he's not going to end up like me." I wanted him to get all the education I'd missed.' These were the fathers who pushed, whose constant message to their children – especially the boys – was that they should make up for the bad fortune of their own past.

'My dad was so keen on education he was down at my primary school every other week demanding that I pass the 11-plus or else,' recalled one boy. Another said: 'My father believed in education like some people do in God. He was forever preaching about the good of education.' It was a familiar story.

At the other end of the scale were those parents baffled by their child's classroom ability. One boy told how his mother phoned the school to check his 11-plus result and still could not believe it. Once it was confirmed her only comment was: 'You'd do better at Triptons.'[5]

Several children's first reaction to the question on how they enjoyed life at County High was to say: 'Well, I didn't think I should have been there in the first place. I didn't fit in. I just wasn't up to it.' And that came from people who finished up in the B stream as well as from those in C and D forms. For many parents getting their children into County High was a mark of achievement in itself. A common remark, I remember from schooldays, among gossiping mothers was: 'He isn't doing very well of course – but at least he's there.' Meaning that he had stepped above the run of the mill secondary modern 'at least'. Here was the charisma of a grammar school seen from the traditional working class viewpoint.

One other notable item was the part played in a child's education by the mother rather than the father. The fathers I have quoted, with only one exception, were typical of the sample because they were given to talking about their children without acting on their behalf. Mothers made most of the day-to-day decisions, many mothers were the driving force behind their children, and it was they who dealt with 'the authorities' whenever necessary. The headmaster saw more mothers than fathers over children's problems, whether to do with academic performance or discipline. Singing festivals, drama productions, career talks, all were the province of mothers. Only the football matches drew an audience of fathers – and that was very few. If mothers were seen to play a prominent part it did not mean that fathers did not have their say. The fireside rumblings and mumblings were translated into firm decisions, or action, by the mother. It would not be fair to conclude that among this working class sample, or indeed from my knowledge of the area, that this was anything like a matriarchal society. Men may have considered education as part of a woman's province simply because they felt ill at ease in dealings with teachers, as might their wives, but they were able to pressure their wives into 'standing in' for them. They were also at work during school hours – though working wives were expected to get time off when needed.

One boy told a story of an argument at home which perfectly illustrates the mother's dilemma in this type of situation:

'I got three detentions one week and the headmaster wrote to my parents saying he'd like to see them about my behaviour. My mother fixed up a time and she went to see him. She said she thought that I had too much homework to do, and it wasn't right, and that's why I kicked up. The head was a bit impolite, talking about lack of discipline coming from the home, and then he said he couldn't see why I should worry about the homework everyone else was doing. Anyway, she climbed down and in the evening, when my father came home, she told him what had happened. She'd worked herself up a bit by then and all my father said was: "You should have walked out." My mum replied: "It's all very well you talking like that, but you wouldn't come. All you do is talk".'

53

The mother in this case appeared to the headmaster as the dominant partner. She had turned up to speak on her son's behalf and when he spoke to her he expected to get a true reaction. But it rarely worked like that. He was an articulate, middle class man and as such could win tacit agreement from tongue-tied mothers who took their real feelings, their anger, back home. Such lack of communication lay at the heart of many of the school's problems. The headmaster's door may have been always open – but was his mind? And were those of the parents? In the ensuing arguments at home it was the school, in the shape of the headmaster, who would eventually take the blame for causing a domestic quarrel. It bred into children a resentment of school which was far from the attitude needed to face the pressures of examination training.

Nearly all the children who turned up to County High on their first day knew at least one other person, either already at the school among the older children or within their common intake. In the first year, when people were mixed in classes without regard to examination ability, cliques began to form. And over the next four years everyone would at some time join, or be on the fringes of, a clique. There was nobody who claimed to have remained entirely outside the scores of tight-knit groups and it was considered to be the normal state of affairs to have such units. It was simply an extension of local home circumstances outside school where in the same street two or three different groups of children would form separate, but not necessarily conflicting, play units. Smaller divisions within nearly 140 pupils – or 70 boys and 70 girls – were also a natural extension of the small unit represented inside the home.

In the early years these cliques were always single sex. Apart from the friendships carried over from primary school, there were the friendships formed on train and bus journeys to and from school. Travellers did not suffer unduly from lack of friends because of their trips, and often the daily confinement of transport produced a more positive forging of fellowship than among those who lived in Dagenham itself. Then there were the cliques of footballers,[6] of car enthusiasts, cyclists, flying fanatics and many more. The fluidity of the cliques and the inter-relation of their members confuse the pattern slightly. Friendships faded throughout the years, interests changed, and the boys and girls mixed considerably more in the later years – the major change in the make-up of cliques between the 11-year-olds who started and the 16 to 18-year-olds who finished. There were furthermore, three groups to illustrate the changing nature of cliques after puberty.

There were the smokers-behind-the-cycle-sheds; the masturbators-behind-the-canteen; and a group of six girls who revealed that they referred to themselves as 'the misfits'. This, said one, was because 'we weren't as aware as all the others. We were more naive.' They felt themselves 'outside' all the other little societies within the society of school. Inclined to be academic, withdrawn, non-sporting and unable to make contact with boys, they retreated into a group. There is no better illustration of the clique system, which even took care to include pupils who felt themselves outsiders.

The cliques, invisible to the casual onlooker and possibly even to the members of staff, and superficially unimportant to the pupils themselves, were rigid with a set of rules rather like a modern British political party: opposite views were made known; conformists to the opinions of the group were made welcome; dissenters were expelled, not always by mutual consent, to join another or form their own; the essence of any group's continuation was compromise since its very existence was bound by the agreement of all its members. The mesh of friendship within school life was therefore based on an individual's search for a mirror of himself ... someone with similar aims and interests, of like temperament, and possibly equal talents as in the cases of sport or academic ability. A pupil's capacity 'to belong' was a crucial factor in his interpersonal relationships at school. Whether he succeeded in forming these playground and classroom friendships was greatly influenced, of course, by his relationships at home.

The novelty of grammar school with its purpose-built classrooms, gowned teachers and inviting new subjects excited the minds of the 11-year-old pupils. Undreamed of vistas opened up before the boys and girls in the first weeks. Even homework was welcomed, occasionally begged for, by pupils wishing to sample the new senior school life and to impress parents in the evening. The honeymoon lasted for a few weeks and when it was over the differences began to show. Pupils from the more stable backgrounds, usually from the upper working class homes, kept their enthusiasm alive, supported by parents who encouraged their children to maintain the pressure, to accept the work and the teaching, to try hard. But not every home was able to stand the added strain of a grammar schoolchild, whose problems seemed too petty, too intrusive, when set against those of the family. These parents resented their child assuming a new position within the household; they mistrusted the book learning; they could not adjust to the fact that their child faced pressures of his own − pressures with which they were unable to cope. Once the school butted in to their own lives, bringing its own sense of mystification, they could not come to terms with the situation. Their resentment manifested itself in a number of ways – some encouraging children not to take work too seriously, some complaining to the headmaster about the pressure forced by his school on the home, and others terrorising children into rejecting their new-found education. One girl was forced to do her homework in the garden shed because her father believed that education was wrong for a girl. This extreme case resulted in the girl putting intense energy into her schoolwork, but parental hostility did not always spur a child to greater effort. Open splits between child and parents were rare, however, and the most common result of parental mistrust was for the child to become apathetic at school.

The first split at school, the streaming division after one year, was for many pupils the major incident of their school life. They thought the decision made then, aged 12, affected the rest of their school careers and consequently their adult lives. Geoffrey West, a pupil placed in the D stream, said: 'From the second year on I was conscious that people thought of us (D stream pupils) as ignorant. I resented it, especially when I saw the carryings-on of the so-called 'bright pupils. The teachers looked down on us as not worth teaching. We must have been bright to have got there in the first place so why were we ignored?' Geoffrey's reaction was to pull away from the school and its activities.

Another boy placed in the D stream, Bill Pearson, spoke of the stigma of being placed in the bottom class. He said: 'I remember being in the hall when they carried out the selection at the beginning of the second year. First, the A class names were called out and they left; then the B; then the C; and then nothing. We weren't mentioned. We just had to accept that we were in the D class. The unmentionables. I never forgot that day.'

A D stream girl, Margaret Duxbury, was particularly bitter at the division. 'At junior school Marion Drake and I were always in the top three in the top class. Then, in the space of one year, it's decided that she is A material and I am D. She got all the advantages and I got every disadvantage going. Streaming must be wrong – the cream always get the best.'

She, and many others in a similar position, believed she would have done far better in the top class of a secondary modern school where she would have received personal GCE coaching,[7] the teaching which all the D class felt they lacked. All the pupils in the D class were conscious of their second-class rating within the school and among the teachers. This is a selection of their feelings about the school, attitudes highly coloured by their selection as D streamers:

> 'The A and B elite was formed in the second and third years and when, in the fourth form, we began to mix across streams it was too late. They had the confidence to do well and we didn't.'

> 'The school hardly had any staff to cope with us. We missed scores of periods over the years. When anyone was sick we missed out.'

> 'You won't find anyone from our class who can say more than five or six words in French let alone understand it or speak it. From the third year on our French lessons were a farce.'

> 'When we were supposed to learn maths in our GCE year the teacher told us that if we didn't give him trouble he wouldn't give us any. He never actually said that, but the hint was clear enough. So we read comics or played battleships[8] while he was off drinking somewhere. No one protested or anything.'

Jim Sanger was a D class pupil – the only one to play in the school football team. He said: 'I was thoroughly ashamed of being in the bottom class. I was superior to everyone in my class. You know what it was like – all the scruffs, all the idiots constantly getting into trouble and never working. They were no good at their work, they were badly behaved, they were no good at sport. I always wished I could have got out of that influence and mixed higher up with the others in the A, B and C forms, friends who were in the team.'

The years spent in the D class gave many a feeling of inferiority. Richard Downside said: 'County High was held in such reverence by my parents as *the* place to go. But when I got there I never felt I belonged. I know it was silly to think so, but then I thought everyone else came from wealthy homes. It was just my way of saying to myself I didn't belong.'

Gary Turner's parents had a similar feeling for the school. 'I didn't think I was cut out for grammar school,' he said, 'but my mum and dad pushed me to go.'

57

Janet King's memories of school were all bad. 'They were the worst days of my life. No joke. The worst.'

Not that the dislike for streaming was confined to the D form. John Elliott said: 'I was hurt by my C rating. I was so unhappy that my mother went to see the headmaster and he promised to put me up to the B stream if I did well in the next two examinations. I came second, then first. But he refused to move me and I reacted to school badly ever afterwards.'

A mistake that may have been, but it is a poignant example of how a sensitive pupil was affected by the streaming system. And it was not an isolated case. The C stream may have had many benefits not accorded the D stream, but the feeling of hopelessness was common. 'Obviously the A and B groups got better teachers,' said David Bacon. 'And only so many out of one school can pass examinations and so many must fail so they gave most help to the people they expected to pass. It was natural.'

One of the most typical attitudes was voiced by Joan Tyson. She said: 'School was a nightmare. There was too much pressure. I never fitted in.'

Joyce Stewart agreed: 'After the first form the pressure was awful. I had easy parents and when I told them I didn't like it they said: "Don't bother then. It isn't worth getting all steamed up about." So I didn't. I don't think I did a week's work all the time I was there.'

I noted several similar stories among C and D pupils – particularly among the girls – and it is not surprising that teachers, faced with stubborn laziness and apathy from pupils, with parental backing, turned a blind eye.

To look at the problem from the other side, consider the two A stream pupils who said they wished they had been anywhere but in the top class. One, Irene Davis, said: 'I struggled so hard to keep up. Everyone round me seemed to find the work so easy and I lost confidence and fell further and further behind.' When she finally was moved down one stream she was so demoralised that she never regained enough assurance to do well.

Glenda James said: 'I felt academically inferior to the people around me.' Yet she was in the A stream throughout her school career. Others felt out of depth in the B stream. The feeling of many that they had arrived at their position by accident was common.

Apart from the traumas created by streaming, the second most oft-voiced claim was among those who thought they could have done better if they had worked harder at school.

'The education was on offer but I never took advantage of it,' said Gerry Kane.

'I only wish I could go back,' said George Jackson. 'I'm sure I'd work instead of playing around.'

Almost a third of those interviewed expressed views very similar to the two above. 'I wouldn't have said it was a bad school,' said Lesley White. 'I couldn't really say that when I didn't do much work. The only way my education could have been improved was by greater effort on my part.'

It must be noted that this attitude, so typical of the sample, can be closely related to their backgrounds. Of the thirty or so people who made this claim only three spoke of genuine parental interest in their education. The division between boys and girls was roughly equal.

David Bacon, a C stream pupil, perhaps came closer to the heart of the problem when he said: 'Class made a real difference. I felt uneasy at that school and as I went on through the years the feeling got worse. You fell into the accepted or the otherwise. I was never accepted.'

Of course, not everyone disliked their stay at the school purely on the grounds of streaming. There were a group of girls, referred to earlier as 'the misfits', for whom school life was intolerable. They shared characteristics which make it highly probable that they would have found any school of County High's size and nature unacceptable. Diana Golding said: 'I was not gregarious so I drew back from people around me. I didn't like most of the people and I had the feeling that most didn't like me.'

Ruth Strong said: 'I was nervous in a classroom. I had an inferiority complex.' [9]

Anita Grundy felt the same way: 'I suppose I was a bit immature. I didn't fit in.'

For three others – Alison Saunders, Christine Barling and Evelyn Newman – the first five years were a terrible ordeal, yet they opted to join the sixth form. All said they were glad they made that choice because the last two years were less lonely and more fulfilling than all the rest.

One or two boys also spoke of being shy and how that prevented them from the full enjoyment others seemed to gain from schooldays. Nearly all the boys and girls who reported introvert tendencies put a lot of effort into their work, ending up with good results.

Naturally, there were those who were untroubled by streaming or shyness and who enjoyed school life. Barry Hammond, an A class pupil, said: 'It was marvellous. There were things that were wrong, but it was the best education anyone could expect in Dagenham. I loved those years.' Mary East, another A streamer, said: 'I wish I was back at school now.' A couple more said the same. Patricia Pope, also an A class student, left after the fifth form, but missed school so much that she rejoined during the lower sixth. 'It was great,' she said.

Few were quite so ecstatic but many others said they had enjoyed their schooldays, if not at the time certainly looking back from ten years on, because of the companionship, the fun and lack of responsibility. Many recalled happy days and delightful incidents . . . like the time Brian Frost threw a satchel across a classroom, hitting a lamp which then fell on Neil Martin's head . . . like the day a teacher ordered the junior football team to do three circuits of the pitch – in a crablike position – for poking fun at the marching boys of the Air Training Corps . . . like the cross-country runs in which some boys stopped halfway for a smoke . . . like all the times when pupils thought they had put one over on teachers – the week of the stink bombs, and the craze for spitting rice through biros converted into peashooters . . . like the summer evenings idled away at nearby Martins Corner just talking about each other. Memories of good times flooded back. Dozens of interviewees said: 'I just didn't realise how good it was until after I'd left.' About eighty people, two thirds of the sample, said they enjoyed their County High schooldays, and it's fair to say that most of them came from upper working class homes. The majority of the third who disliked school came from the homes of the less prosperous working class with parents who showed little interest in their education. Views were in nearly every case emotive, and corresponded in great measure as to how successful they were in their final examinations.

Very few had ideas about how the running of the school could have been improved. On the question of curriculum, I found little support for the introduction of current affairs discussions. There was a lobby on behalf of economics and a number of attacks on the narrowness of the religious teaching – unsurprising when there were so few churchgoers among the sample. Several girls were angered by the lack of courses which they claimed could have led them straight into jobs, saying that secondary modern girls taught commercial subjects had an unfair advantage on leaving. There were many cries for 'a more general education', without specific ideas about what that might include or exclude, and a body of opinion which considered examinations a poor method of evaluating ability. Even among those pupils who became teachers there was no real insight into the ways in which County High's educational system could have been changed for the better.

People were much more forthcoming on the problems of discipline. The majority thought the rules just and their administration fair – but there were some claims of victimisation, particularly in the lower streams, and among girls there were harsh words about the pettiness of wearing school uniforms. Discipline seemed to many to be a virtue and the favourite teachers named by nearly everyone embodied such a view, noted as they were for their rigorous attention to the observance of the school rules by pupils. 'The good teachers,' said Jeff Jones, 'got obedience by their manner. They got everyone to listen and we were scared not to. The bad teachers just couldn't keep us quiet so we larked around and never learnt a thing.'

Donald Abbott thought the mixture of discipline and humour made all the difference to children's appreciation of a teacher. It was, he agreed, a difficult balance to achieve, but those who succeeded gained the lasting regard of generations of pupils.

'That —— was a bastard,' said Paul Lee, 'but I look back and know he was brilliant at his job. He got us to listen . . . to really pay attention. That was the thing. He gave me hell but it did me good.'

Barry Hammond thought the same master was 'too good for County High,' a strange choice of phrase from a boy who considered there was not enough discipline in the school and a lack of respect for teachers and prefects. Control of pupils was the essential factor in giving a good education, he said.

Danny Reynolds gave the majority opinion: 'At the time I was in school I was scared to put a foot out of line. The headmaster terrified me, though I never actually spoke to him. But looking back it wasn't so bad. I never had nightmares about discipline. It did me good to learn of bit of respect. After I left I met people in jobs who didn't know how to behave. They'd been allowed to do as they liked in secondary modern schools. They weren't fitted out to face working life.'

Under the terms of grammar school entrance parents agreed to keep their children at the school until they had completed their fifth form year at the age of 16. However, children had the right to leave at 15 – then the national minimum school leaving age – if their parents were prepared to pay the sum of £10. This process, known as 'buying out', was a primitive exercise in attempting to make parents understand the step they were taking. It also had the Judas ring about it, this selling of a child's educational prospects for so many pieces of silver, and every £10 handed to the headmaster represented, to his mind, a waste of four years for him and his staff. The primary object of grammar school was to educate pupils up to the point of taking their GCE O–level examinations. Only one of the nine people I interviewed who left aged 15 did so without an attempt by the head to discourage the move, and that was because the girl was pregnant.[10]

Four boys and four girls left voluntarily after their fourth form year. A few others who stayed until the fifth said they too would have left if their parents would have allowed them. Seven of the early leavers came from council houses, four of them from Dagenham's Becontree Estate.

It is an over-simplification to say that all seven sets of parents took little interest in their children's education, but with one exception, it is true that the parents did not offer good advice, did not coerce their children, or had worries which transcended child educational problems. Marion Fryer was determined to leave at the earliest possible opportunity, in spite of being in the A stream, because examinations made her extremely nervous and the worry grew with every exam. Her parents, she said, 'never thought education very important.'

Angela Harper, Marion's classmate and close friend, also left at 15 under some influence, she claims, from Marion. Angela said: 'Both my parents thought I was doing well at the school and they were sorry when I told them I was going to leave. But they could not overcome my obsession. I just had to leave.'

Jennifer Long never expected to pass her 11-plus, and found academic life difficult at the grammar school, ending up in the C stream. She left 'to earn money', without a lot of parental questioning of her decision.

Gordon Huntley enjoyed school for the first two years. He was placed in the B stream, liked the work and took an active part in sports activities. His father took a lot of interest in his education, making Gordon nervous about failure and even more troubled about the reprimand that followed failure. 'I cheated in an exam once because I knew nothing about the paper. I got caught and it was put on my report,' he said. 'I was so scared of my father knowing that I got my mum to sign the report and cover up for me.' From the age of 13 all Gordon wanted to do was leave. 'I got bored I suppose. I got fed up with it all. I detested going to school each day.'

Pauline Slade was also in the B form. 'I was timid,' she said, 'and teachers didn't take much of an interest in quiet people like me.' Exams terrified her and she felt under a lot of undue stress which she felt unable to articulate to anyone. The only relief from the strain was to leave as soon as possible. Eight years after she left Pauline wrote to the school requesting a job reference and was amazed to read on its return the phrase: 'Considered suitable for further education.' She said: 'If only they had stressed this to me when I was 14 years old and given me the confidence I lacked it may well have changed my whole future.'

For Derek Lever and Ronald Dwyer there were home problems that had a marked effect on their decisions to leave. Derek lived with his divorced mother and grandparents. When he was fourteen his grandfather died, making an already critical family budget still worse. He saw in himself the bread-winner and went straight to work the day summer holidays began after the end of the fourth form. There was no argument at home. 'I was always left to do what I liked,' he said.

From the age of six Ronald Dwyer was aware that his mother was very ill. She grew worse over the years and finally died, when he was 13, of cancer. Despite the inevitability of her death it came as a blow to the boy and his father. Already unhappy at school because of 'feeling different', Ronald said: 'School for me was 75 per cent laughs marred by misery.' He wanted to earn money, to gain independence, to escape his home, the school, his past. Leaving could not come quick enough.

The eighth early leaver was Steven Ayres, who lived in a private house in Hornchurch, the son of a printer. Steven decided to follow his father into the trade – virtually the only way to enter – and to do so meant taking up an apprenticeship at 15. He had not enjoyed school life, explaining: 'I was an introvert and I didn't like sport. So I was one of a pretty detached group. Even then I was probably the least social of the group. I hated school.'

Three of the eight were to regret their decision although it took some time for two to come to terms with their change of mind. Gordon Huntley realised straightaway, however, on joining the Gas Board, for he was immediately required to go to day and night classes to pass GCE exams. 'What a stupid thing it was to leave early when all I did was study for the very exams I would have had to have taken had I stayed at school.'

Jennifer Long says she took a long time to discover she had made a big mistake, and Angela Harper said it was five years before she realised that leaving had robbed her of a good occupational start. She had always had an aptitude for school work and 'for personal enjoyment' sat and passed four GCEs at college when aged 24.

Whether there were, or were not, regrets it has to be said that looking at the overall picture of fourth and fifth form leaving the early leavers do not appear to have unduly suffered from missing the last year, except in terms of believing that they did. Three appeared to have had the potential to have done very well at GCE, going on to sixth form, and possibly, university. The theory is, however, invalid in that several pupils who stayed on to the fifth form also did not realise their potential, so there is little guarantee that leaving early dramatically affected their lives. The important factor was their environment, not their education, yet none of them were able to see this. All were critical of the school – 'mediocre', 'awful', 'hopeless' were their summaries – but none thought their parents were to blame.

From the beginning of our time at County High we were told of the distant examinations that would decide our futures. These exams, we were reminded, were our opportunity to escape our present situations and enter the professional world. One master had a habit of telling his classes that they represented part of the country's top 23 per cent and it was about time they acted like it unless, that is, they wished to join the 77 per cent in the bottom drawer. Pupils in grammar schools were among the chosen few. To stay on top, teachers were fond of telling children, you had to work hard at school and pass exams . . . GCE O–levels. Eight was the maximum on offer; five were needed to go on to sixth form study – the study that could carry someone to college or university. With an increasing fervour as the terms slipped away into years the message was drummed into us. If you don't want to waste your life work hard to pass your GCEs. No pupil can have been in any doubt by the start of the fourth form why he was at the school for this was the term everyone chose their eight GCE subjects. From that moment on all of us were aware of our individual targets.

Ninety-six of this sample sat their O–levels in the early summer of 1963 after showing their abilities in the winter at what were called 'mock GCEs'. Success at mocks determined whether a person would sit for the subject. I could obtain no figures for those mock exams but I was able to measure the degree of success in the true GCEs. The best way to present them is stream by stream. The 24 A stream pupils who sat the exams passed in 140 subjects, giving an average per child of almost six passes. The 26 in the B class passed in 131 subjects – an average of five. The 27 C streamers passed in 99 subjects – an average of about 3.5. And the 19 in the D stream passed in 33 – an average of 1.75. The girls, overall, performed better than the boys by a difference of about one pass on average. These figures can be seen in two ways, either as a tribute to the success of a streaming system which had foreseen pupils' potential at the beginning of the second year, or as a sad reflection on a practice which allowed the bottom two streams to fall below the O–level pass average in the top classes of surrounding secondary modern schools. [11]

Only two pupils in the D stream obtained five passes. In the C stream nine pupils got five or more passes; in the B, there were 17 with five or more passes; and in the A, only four of the 25-strong sample failed to achieve the five-pass standard.

Unsurprisingly, the D stream was not represented in the lower sixth, although three boys did stay on for one extra year in the fifth form to re-sit O–level examinations. They were not put into the lowest stream during this additional year and all prospered. Jim Sanger, [12] who passed two GCEs in 1963 gained five more passes a year later, to leave with a creditable seven; Gary Turner left with three after failing every exam the first time round; and Christopher Kirk finally got six. All three boys had parental encouragement which led them to stay on when all their classmates had gone.

One boy from the C class and two from the B also returned to the fifth form to re-take GCE O–levels. The C boy, Peter Waters, went on to the sixth form while the B pair left after adding to their O–level totals.

Three boys and one girl from the C stream took up sixth form study, as did four boys and two girls from the B stream and seven boys and four girls from the A stream. But why did so many who had done well at O-levels leave school? Why were so many of those leavers girls? The first question produces a variety of answers: for some, home economics demanded another wage earner; for others, school had not provided a pleasant base for five years and they could not find enthusiasm to withstand two more; for many, gaining independence was uppermost in their thoughts; and for a few, there had been every intention to return but during the six-week summer holidays they saw friends striding proudly off to work and followed suit. The answer to the second question has no such diversity: girls in working class families were not encouraged to seek education beyond 16. Some went off to college to take one-year commercial courses; others took the best job their GCEs could win them. One or two said they seriously considered staying on but could not face the discipline when so many other girls of their age were enjoying independence, the independence that allowed them to put on make-up every morning, to dress in the latest fashion, to carry handbags in place of satchels.

There were many more, of course, who left with only one or two 0–levels to their credit. Eight got no passes at all – six from the D stream and two from the C. Most of them were bitter about their schooldays. Geoffrey West, for instance, looked back in anger at his education: 'I got a very bad deal from the start. Being in the bottom class meant being taught by clowns. I was over the moon when the time came to leave.'

It was the same for Patrick Taylor. 'I hated every minute, possibly because I wasn't doing well. My parents expected me to succeed but I now see that they could have done more to help. I lacked drive. I was a shy boy in a class where there was no discipline. The school was no good for me. I think I would have done better elsewhere.'

Not fitting into the slot was a common complaint. Linda Croft applied a certain twisted logic to her 'feeling different' from others which she thought compensated her initial uneasiness. 'I was lucky to be in the D class. I felt inferior to people in the first year but once we were streamed I felt safe in the D class. I never did well but then lots of those around me didn't either.'

Thirteen more pupils, seven boys and six girls, left with only one or two passes. Among them was John Elliot, who considered the whole basis of the schooling wrong because only those who did well at the beginning 'got the benefit of a real grammar school education'. The fact that he did not begin well and got no reward for doing better later took away his will to succeed in the final exams.

Mark Willis thought that since the school's main aim appeared to him to be to prepare people for exams it was rough on those, like him, in the lower streams, who did not get even that training.

Julia Kilbey was in the B stream but could not keep up with the workrate demanded of her. 'They didn't stop for slow ones like me and I found the going hard. I really looked forward to getting out.'

None of these people could demand jobs by virtue of their GCE passes, so they were forced to hunt for the best and hope that things might get brighter one way or another in the future. They could, of course, continue to study at evening classes to make up for their schoolday losses.

Among the rest of the fifth form leavers 38 gained three, four or five passes. More interestingly eleven passed in six, seven or eight subjects. It is unlikely that so many – more than ten per cent – would have left school, having achieved such passes, at this stage if from middle class homes, and their reasons for leaving bear this out.

Alan Phillips, an A streamer, got eight O–levels. He said: 'As the youngest of five children my parents didn't think they could have afforded to send me to university. They didn't know about grants or anything like that. I regret leaving and now wish I had gone to university.'

Brenda Ford was also in the A stream. She passed seven GCEs and looked forward to sixth form study. She could not be any other than aware of parental hostility since she had been forced to revise for her exams in the garden shed because her father considered education for girls improper. Her efforts were scorned by her family, her results greeted without interest and when she announced that she would be returning to school her father refused to allow it, deciding instead that she should go out and earn money, 'to help the whole family'. Brenda's family was one of the poorest I met on the survey. Her father was persistently sick, and she felt obliged to go to work.

Vivienne Kidd was refused permission by parents to stay on at school. She said: 'I wish now I'd kicked up a fuss.' Norma Gregson's parents did not, she said, take much interest in whether she stayed or went to work. Cathy Richards, who got seven passes sprinkled with top grades, was also left to make up her own mind by her parents while Cathy's friends tried to urge her to stay on. 'But I just suddenly rebelled,' she recalled. 'I didn't like the way the teachers and the others were pushing me to go to university.' So she left.

Keith Lester got six passes and was another who said his parents could not afford to keep him at school. At each extreme, from the exam failures to successes, the thread runs true: children were subject to environmental pressures which decided their educational fate. The school, even if it had wished to, was powerless to overcome the parental attitude.

Sixth form life was a world away from the earlier years. Tony Newton summed it up: 'The last two years at school it was like a bloody holiday camp. It was great.' Twenty-two of the 96 people who sat O–levels stayed on for sixth form study, yet only seven of those were girls. The fifth form A stream had twice as many girls as boys, and the girls overall performed better in O–levels than boys. Yet only four A stream girls stayed on, while of the nine boys in the same stream just two left. The sixth form was supplemented by the arrival of pupils from secondary modern schools who had succeeded at O–levels, the so-called failures who had come in from the cold. In this group there were three girls, from the all-girls Eastbrook School in Dagenham, and one boy from an Ilford school, Mayfield. Of the 22, one boy left after his lower sixth year because, he said, of a difference of opinion with the headmaster. This row appears to have blown up over the boy's infatuation with a girl, and despite the school's co-educational basis and relaxed sixth form it was not over-liberal in its attitude towards petting in the corridors. It was a decision the boy was later to regret.

Nearly all those who stayed at school until they were 18 or 19 had parents who were ambitious for their child's advancement, or who gave them complete freedom of choice. In this latter category was Alison Saunders, finally the most successful of all the sixth formers in her academic achievements. She said: 'My parents gave me independence. I always planned to go to university and as far as I was concerned that was what I was going to do. I disregarded my parents and they did the same to me. I existed as an individual.'

Said Tony Newton: 'My parents made all the right noises, but they didn't really encourage me.'

Kenneth Bird spoke for the majority when he told how his parents 'encouraged without pushing'. They believed it was right for him to take his education as far as possible and provided a stable home background. 'They did all they could to give me the opportunity,' he said.

The sixth formers had their minds concentrated on a new set of examinations, the GCE Advanced levels. They began their two-year stay by deciding which three subjects to study, and most were naturally looking beyond school at this stage to university entrance. With small numbers and a wide diversity of aims and hopes there were bound to be disappointments. Timothy Simmons had been in the C stream, managing to pass seven O–levels, but his achievement won scant recognition from the head mathematics teacher. He said: 'I got one grade below that the teacher considered necessary to study at A–level. So I was forced to give up maths – the one subject I really wanted to take. When I complained the headmaster said I should take the subjects chosen for me or leave.' It was a harsh decision. A good grade at O–level mathematics from the C stream was an excellent result, and few can doubt that with an A stream teacher he might have done much better. This narrow-minded judgement on the boy's ability was to change the course of his life.

One or two others felt they had chosen the wrong subjects later in their sixth form career, but that was quite different. Most got what they wanted.

With only three main subjects, the new sixth formers found themselves with an abundance of free time, some of which was taken up with arts and crafts subjects, some by sport, and not a little by discussion, either formally, under guidance in a classroom, or just among the pupils in their room or in the corner of the library. The old cliques of the fifth form were split asunder, and in the sixth form new ones formed, based mainly on the similarity of study. The zoology and botany group, boys and girls, became a tight-knit formation, for example, as did the economists.

And in the upper sixth year all but a few of the sample became prefects, giving them minimal responsibility but a new role to play in the school, and particularly in their relation to the younger pupils. It also changed their status in the eyes of the teachers. 'They became more like equals – taking part in our jokes and encouraging us to enjoy our free time. They also helped the subject they were teaching to come alive. It wasn't such a hard slog any more,' said Malcolm Dove.

In some cases teachers not only *advised* on free time activities but *demonstrated*. Peter Waters said: 'Teachers were like mates in the sixth form. I even went drinking with one a couple of evenings. It made all the difference. It made those last years really great.'

Discipline was not altogether relaxed however. Three boys were refused prefectships because they would not get their long hair cut. All three recalled the incident, but only Timothy Simmons was still indignant at the headmaster's ultimatum. He thought the work pressures in the last year were too important for such a minor point to become an issue, and he blamed the headmaster for allowing it to reach that state. Timothy was one of the few who found the going tough in the sixth form, but he did have two major clashes with authority. For most, the two years were a memory of gaiety and freedom in which work became a secondary problem. Some of the boys formed a pop group and played at evening dances in the school hall. Meeting outside school hours in large groups – a rare occurrence except for football in the earlier years – became fairly common. Social life was an extension of school in a way which would have been impossible in the years before when primary school and street friendships were continued. With those friends at work, discovering new friends themselves, the sixth formers looked to their own select group for socialising.

With one or two exceptions work did not suffer unduly from this new way of life. Rod Mason was one of the leading lights of the pop group and became so enamoured with its activities, and with a girl he met while playing at a local dance hall, that he began to ignore his work. He passed only one A–level, thereby ending his chance of going on to university. 'When I failed I knew why and so did my father. He was bitter. But I was courting and I just couldn't knuckle down any more. I had to change all my plans.' Stewart Allen failed all his exams. He said: 'I don't think those two years were wasted though. It had been a marvellous experience and it was a wrench to leave because I knew I wouldn't work in an atmosphere like that again.'

Having acclimatised himself to the discipline of pressure from teachers in the first five years Leslie Wood could never come to terms with the self-discipline necessary for sixth form work. 'I became lazy. I avoided lectures,' he said. 'I think the education was good until the fifth, but then I never felt pushed. I guess I rebelled. My parents didn't like it, of course, and there was lot of friction at home.' He passed ten O–levels but only one 'A'.

These three cases – of Mason, Allen and Wood – illustrate one of the major problems facing teachers today: how to treat the older pupils. Many adolescents like these who are still at school do not consider themselves as older children but as young adults. Perhaps they are incorrect in their own assertions, but the conflict of roles is there nevertheless. If confronted with an inflexible system – i.e. a school where teachers can only afford to concentrate their energies on those children willing to work – then the 'rebellious' few will not get the expert advice they need. In all three cases parents were unable to guide their children, in spite of their encouragement and sympathy, because they had no experience themselves in a situation of that kind. The school offered no help because its staff were not trained to cope with this changing of roles that inevitably occurs in adolescents, and which seems to occur at earlier ages with each emerging generation.

Neil Martin, Susan Kingley and Mary East all passed in only one subject but none had their eyes on a university place and had stayed on into the sixth form because they seemed unsure about stepping into the outside world. Said Neil: 'I can't remember being happier than when I was at school. Life gets too complicated when you grow up.'

Mary East enjoyed her sixth form so much she still, eight years after leaving, organises get-togethers for a group of sixth form girls. She thought the early schooling was 'too formal' in tone, and was aimed at providing university and college students, but added: 'It was a very good sixth. That's what keeps us meeting. All the memories.'

Another who left with one A–level was Peter Waters. He was one of those who failed to achieve good enough results in his first sitting at O–levels and so stayed on an extra year in the fifth, obtaining six passes. He was therefore one year behind his old classmates and one year older than his new ones during his sixth form years. It was a situation many might have disliked but not Peter. Having been one of the school's most outstanding sportsmen – a goal-scoring footballer, a wicket-taking cricketer and record-breaking sprinter – and a House captain during each year of his school life, it was no surprise when he was made head boy in his final year. His popularity among the boys was matched by his attraction for girls, and Peter's romantic involvements were as frequent as his sporting successes. He said: 'I enjoyed myself in the sixth especially, but then I enjoyed school altogether.' He was an only child, given much help and advice from parents. 'They were really great,' he said. 'We got on together incredibly well and we had this wonderful repartee. It was a very close and special relationship. I knew more about life than other boys around me in school. I drank before they did and I went into betting shops before them. I always had money, too. Other boys would come to me for advice. I seemed older than them.' This role of father-figure, in which he revelled, was to influence his choice of career.

Of the other 14 sixth formers, five got two A–levels, eight got three and one girl got five. Their aims were further education rather than quick money, and their results provided them with the opportunity to pursue that goal. These were the 14 stars from the 96 beginners, the group who came out from County High with the top honours. Not all of them were enamoured with their education or with the school.

Robin Edwards, an A streamer who got eight O–levels and two A–levels, said: 'On hindsight I suppose worse things do happen. But school never stimulated me. I thought it petty in its discipline; lacking in current affairs discussion and, worst of all, I got bad advice on what subjects I should take. I should have studied applied maths at A–level. Only when I left did I realise that if there had been expert help over careers then I wouldn't have suffered as I did later.'

Timothy Simmons, the boy refused permission to take A–level mathematics, was not so much misled as forced to take the wrong path. It is hardly surprising that he should he embittered about the school, though he confined his comments at one point in our talk to the general tone of the education offered him rather than its

71

detailed effects on him personally. 'The main problem was that the teachers had never got away from academic life so they could not possibly help children to see the world outside. Careers advice, which I now see as of major importance, was an incidental amusement at school. I realise there are many diverse careers a child can follow, especially having had the benefit of grammar school learning, but it is inexcusable that they did nothing at all of any real value. I suppose they thought that there were so many aspects to consider they wouldn't bother.'

Terry Warner was one of many enraged by the emphasis on sport. 'For people like me who were forced to play football and who were bored by all physical effort it was a hopeless school. Were footballers forced to enter into discussions on politics or the role of trade unions? Of course they weren't. The stimulation of thought at County High was nil. Overall, school was a pain.'

The freedom of the sixth form could not compensate for the ordeal of the first five years for Evelyn Newman. She entered enthusiastically into sport and off-stage drama assistance, but her C stream rating made her feel inferior to many others. Her good O–level results, obtained by hard work and an application aided by her classroom shyness, convinced her that she was as good as her A stream friends. She therefore prospered in the sixth, passing three A–levels. She said: 'I didn't enjoy the early years. Instead of being allowed to develop as people, we were taught to take exams. Educationally, it was very conservative. We had no general education, nothing on politics for instance.' She also touched on another point, the school's strange double standard in its attitude to girls. 'One small thing that upset me in the sixth was that I was not allowed to take woodwork. If it was all right for the boys to do cookery why couldn't I do their subject?'

The early years also distressed Christine Barling. She found some solace in the sixth, but did not allow the relaxed atmosphere to end her dedication to work. She gained two more O–levels to add to the eight she obtained at the end of the fifth form, and three A–levels. She said she 'had reservations' about the merits of school but did not elucidate, except to say that she considered the teaching of religious knowledge should have 'gone further than Christianity,' and there should have been some form of sex education and current affairs discussions.

Kenneth Bird was the only one of the group to speak up on behalf of the lower forms. He was in the A stream but concluded that 'life seemed bad' in the C and D classes. He thought the whole system of education was wrong. 'We were asked to choose subjects too early in life. The choice was too narrow. Then all we did with those subjects was to learn them for exams. And exams were ridiculous.' Kenneth stayed on for an extra year in the sixth and left to go to university with three A–levels, as did Malcolm Dove. He spent his first years at school with a feeling of inferiority, in spite of his academic competence, because of speaking with a stutter and not shining at sport. 'I felt insignificant – one of the out-crowd.' But his extrovert involvement with the pop group in the sixth form changed his image and bolstered his confidence, although only the intervention of his teacher managed to stop him from giving up his schoolwork at one point. Despite this, Malcolm considered the teaching standard generally low and later thought that his education had been 'pretty poor' in comparison with that given to other university undergraduates.

Alison Saunders left school at 19 with eight O–levels and five A–levels, a remarkable achievement by any standard, but made even more so by the fact that all were high grade passes. She, too, only enjoyed her sixth form years, having disliked what she called the petty discipline of the first five years and having developed what amounted to a paranoia about sport. 'During double games lessons I would sometimes sit in the toilets to avoid it. I just never could get to like competitive sport, and I detested all that went with it – the one-upmanship, the bit about being chosen to represent, all that effort. I loved compensating for my deficiencies at sport by doing well at exams so I achieved a good exam technique. But at school you couldn't beat the sports thing. If you shone at hockey and failed exams you could hold your head up high. Passing exams with honour may have made you popular with teachers but it didn't among most of the pupils.' This feeling threw her into the arms of the 'misfit clique' during her early years but the break-up of that tight-knit group in the sixth drew her into the more socially outgoing throng and she became known for a dry wit. Looking back, Alison believed that teachers had had it in their power to make the school worthwhile by their individual appeal, but she thought only two worth a mention. One, formerly a university lecturer, greatly influenced her final years, embodying much in her personality that Alison found admirable. 'I wanted to be like her,' she said.

Barry Hammond was one of those who wished he could go back to school because he enjoyed the experience so much, claiming also that it was the best education Dagenham could offer. But he was critical of the system and concerned at the omissions in the curriculum. 'I don't think we should have been restricted to taking just eight subjects at O–levels. I'd like to have taken fifteen. It was an arbitrary way of governing the rest of our lives. There shouldn't be any segregation of subjects at any age.' This was a view shared by no one else, although it is an extension of the argument that deciding on eight subjects aged 14 is too early a demand on the developing child. Barry became head boy in the last year, chosen for his success at examinations, enthusiasm on the sports field and a wide interest in other school activities from writing poetry in the school magazine to forming a weight-lifting club. He came from a private house in Dagenham and his parents, he said, were 'terrifically encouraging, very pro success'. This was borne out by the progress of two younger brothers who both joined County High and did extremely well in their work. On one speech day, Barry recalled, he and his two brothers won six prizes between them. Barry said almost the same as Peter Waters – the boy who was to become head boy the following year. 'After the first couple of years it became accepted by the others that I was superior. People in my class came to me for advice.'

Marion Drake, who became head girl, was less critical of her schooling and more equivocal about her role as leader. She said she suffered from 'personality conflicts' and was surprised when she was chosen. Again, success both at sport and in exams were the major reasons for her emergence as head girl. The other four of this group all claimed to have enjoyed their schooldays and did not have more than minor qualms about its quality. Paul Lee said he would have preferred pupils to have been guided into the daily habit of reading a newspaper, for example.

All 14 came from fairly similar backgrounds, though seven lived in private houses, six in council accommodation and one in 'a house that came with my dad's job'. [13] All were well behaved in school. Nine said they read a lot outside their normal schoolwork demands during their spare time. Thirteen were in favour of current affairs discussions being an integral part of the school curriculum, a number giving instances of the lack of knowledge about politics and modern history about which they had been embarrassed at some stage of their adult lives.

To conclude this schooldays' saga let me simply add that of the 112 pupils covered in this section six went directly from County High to university, four joined teachers' training colleges, and one went to a college of further education. Some years later, three more went to teachers' training college, one entered university and another took a full-time polytechnic course.

United We Earn

The daunting problems presented by the drawing together of all the strands into a readable format led me to the conclusion that it was necessary to divide this section. In adult life the main difference in influences and direction was sex, so I will pursue the lives of men and women in separate sections. Let me stress that this division has no foundation in anti-feminism. Quite the reverse, for it will become evident that dealing with women as a separate case results in a more positive advocacy of the cause of women's liberation than might have been otherwise possible.

However, before the split is made, let me provide some general information relevant to both groups. The children who joined County High lived in and around the Dagenham area. At the point the previous chapter finished the teenagers were about to leave school. Now I move on, ten years for most and seven for some sixth formers, to the present. First, let us see where all these schoolchildren have moved to since their schooldays.

TABLE 1
Geographical distribution of sample

Home areas	Boys	Girls	Totals
Dagenham	8	9	17
Hornchurch & Upminster	4	6	10
Rest of Essex	22	28	50
London	1	3	4
Midlands & East Anglia	4	1	5
North of England	3	0	3
West Country	2	3	5
Rest of England	9	5	14
Abroad	1	3	4
Totals	54	58	112

Seventeen remain in the area which used to be known as the Borough of Dagenham. Four are unmarried and are still living with their parents; five have become house owners, four live in local council accommodation and only three continue to rent houses on the Becontree Estate. One lives in a flat provided by his employers over the grocery shop of which he is manager. There are two main reasons why those who married stayed: firstly, the wish to keep close to their parents; secondly, the impossibility of raising enough money to buy a house.

The case of Danny Reynolds and Helen Spicer is an example of the dilemma facing a young married couple with a low income. They were in the same class throughout their school lives but did not get together until some months after leaving. They both took jobs which they gave up after six months or so out of frustration and boredom. Both joined insurance brokerages in the City where the money was relatively low but the promotional prospects looked good. Danny tried four firms before settling down, while Helen stayed at her second choice for a couple of years. They married when they were 20, and moved in with Danny's parents, a three-bedroom house on the Becontree Estate, saving up for a house of their own. But they just could not save enough and were about to enter the market when house prices began to spiral.

'To have bought a house at a reasonable price would have meant moving so far out into Essex that I couldn't have afforded to pay the mortgage and my train fare, plus I couldn't have stood the aggravation of travelling,' said Danny. Eventually they were offered a council house of their own on the Estate, which they had to accept reluctantly. Helen gave up work to have a baby, putting another strain on resources, and then Danny was told that his firm were planning to move their offices out of London to Ipswich. They discovered that their chance of transferring a council house with someone in Ipswich was slight and soon found that house prices were outside their range. Both want to leave Dagenham. 'I'm not keen on it here even though my relatives live close,' said Danny. He took a part-time job in the evening at a local pub to try and raise capital and said he hoped for a benevolent turn of mind from his employers. He said: 'My wages are frozen and I'm stuck. I need to move for my job and I can't. I don't know what I'm going to do.'

Three others told similar stories of attempts to save that fell short of the target. All wanted to leave Dagenham. Said Maureen Crowe: 'I'd much rather live in the country. We're waiting to hear about a new town swop. We could never buy a home of our own now.'

Margaret Duxbury, on the other hand, said she and her husband had been offered a chance to leave their Dagenham house for an East Anglian new town but they rejected it. She liked being near her mother, and in the traditional working class manner, her mother looked after her children during the day while she went out to work in the office of a local factory.

This convenient arrangement is also used by Marion Drake, who lives on the Estate. She said: 'I don't think I'll stay in Dagenham forever. But I've mellowed to the place and having adjusted to it I don't dislike it too much.'

The table reveals that the majority have moved into Essex. Most have bought houses on little estates that sprung up on the edge of villages during the mid-Sixties as developers realised the house-buying potential of the young emergent, affluent, working class. Many moved much further into rural Essex than they had planned, but prices forced them to accept the move, sometimes miles from railway stations on the line to London. One man, Leslie Wood, lives ten miles from the nearest station at Colchester – some 60 miles from London – and works in Hammersmith, to the west of London, a prodigious daily journey which takes him about two-and-a-half hours each way. Others in mid-Essex face similar travelling rigours.

Those who live in the North and West Country are generally those who left their homes for university and college after leaving school. And 'the rest of England' covers those who moved across the Thames into Kent or who moved just out of Essex into Hertfordshire and Bedfordshire. Although I contacted only four people who have emigrated, I discovered that one other boy in the year was thought to be in Australia, and three of the girls I interviewed were about to follow suit. [1]

In the main, people have moved away from their childhood districts and away from their parents. It is equally true that many have moved away from their working class origins to hold a status within society vastly different from that of their parents. The tanker driver's daughter is doing research into cancer; the crane driver's son is a stockbroker's assistant; the supermarket odd job man's daughter is an occupational therapist; the Ford sheet metal worker's son is employed at the factory as an executive accountant. The chart beginning on page 80 reveals many similar comparisons.

Not only are their houses in different places, but the children of council house tenants have become men and women of property. Seventy-five of the sample lived in either council or rented accommodation while at school, now only 25 do so. And of those, three still live with their parents, four others are single and rent flats, two more are about to buy houses, and two live in accommodation provided by employers. As we have seen, most of those who remain in council houses would prefer to purchase if given the chance – an aim which not all parents, even if the opportunity had been theirs, would have shared.

The houses are different also in style. Very few parents had cars, let alone a garage, but their children's houses have garages which form the central component of their new homes. After visiting scores of houses whose prominent feature was a garage I began to believe that motor cars themselves supported the home. Unlike the fenced-in front gardens of Dagenham these houses have 'open plan' fronts, 'to get all the children together and let all the local dogs mess on every lawn,' said Sally Bailey.

Inside, the sparse furnishings were a notable contrast with the muddle of their parents' homes. The through-lounge with a picture window at one end was a hallmark of every new home. Furniture was 'modern' without being fashionable, and the three-piece suite was positioned round an electric fire, often in spite of a perfectly adequate central heating system. Colour televisions abounded and stereo record-players were growing in popularity. Shelves contained sets of books in imitation leather, but magazines and newspapers were rarely on view. Ornaments, if there were any, were of the large and chunky variety, and clutter occurred only in those homes where there were children.

There were twenty-nine mothers and thirteen fathers among the ninety-one married people in this sample (including one woman who was divorced); and five in the twenty-one who were single were on the verge of marrying when I met them. The eldest children were of junior school age, but most were at the nursery stage with its attendant problems, mainly the need for constant attention. I carried out one interview with a woman who was still in bed after having her first child. Her mother was on hand, despite the 20 miles separating their homes, and I was given tea and biscuits at the bedside. This sort of hospitality was offered by nearly everyone. 'Now before we talk,' a woman would ask, 'what do you want – tea or coffee?' It was rare to be offered alcohol, though I did sample home-made wines on one occasion and a fine malt whiskey on another. It was not uncommon for men to invite me to the local 'for a quick one later on'.

Food and drink seemed to base the talks on an easier footing for the interviewees, breaking down the barriers they felt existed. Among those who could not remember me there was suspicion and sometimes hostility, not openly articulated but shown in the aggressiveness of their replies. To a lesser degree some of those who did know me were wary, particularly the women. Who was he, I imagined them to say to their partners after I had left, to ask all those questions? The most typical response after completing the interviews was: 'Can I ask you something now? What do you hope to gain from all this information? It's going to be a funny sort of a book.'

The statistics of social mobility – lists of comparative salary scales, graphs of material achievement, registers of occupational differences – cannot do justice to these people, their problems and their lifestyles. Their words and my impressions, however imperfect in translation, will paint the picture over the numbers. To help readers link the schoolchild to the adult, here is a reference chart showing their development during the ten years.

MEN

Name	Father's occupation	School Stream	School Exam Results	After-school education	Job 1973–74	Annual Salary 1974
Donald Abbott	Hospital buyer	B	6–O	—	Store executive	£2,250
Peter Adams	Printer	LD	4–O	Failed accounts	Telephone engineer	£1,565
Stewart Allen	Postman	C	6–O	Pub. health Dip.	Pub. health inspector	£2,670
John Andrews	Ford inspector	B	7–O, 2–A	B.Sc.(Agric.)	Agric. machine res'ch	£2,500
Steven Ayres	Printer	B	N/T*	—	Clerk	£1,750
David Bacon	Ford foundryman	C	Nil	—	Bookie's manager	£3,500
Michael Barton	Recreation mgr.	C	1–O	5–O, Pub.health Dip.	Pub. health inspector	£2,680
Kenneth Bird	Electrical eng.	A	8–O, 3–A	Failed degree course	Comp. programmer	£1,625
Raymond Crouch	Clerk	C	4–O	—	Policeman	£1,500
John Douglas	Research eng.	LLD	9–O	—	Insur. co. supervisor	£1,950
Malcolm Dove	Factory super.	B	7–O, 3–A	Ph.D.	Leukaemia researcher	£2,000
Richard Downside	Painter	D	3–O	1–O, HNC eng.	Ford cost analyst	£2,500
Colin Drew	Nurse	D	4–O	—	Bank clerk	£2,000
Ronald Dwyer	Security guard	D	N/T*	—	Shop manager	£3,000
Robin Edwards	Clerk of works	A	8–O, 2–A	Eng. degree course	Student	Grant
John Elliott	Maintenance eng.	C	1–O	6–O, 2–A, account'cy	Financial analyst	£3,150
Brian Frost	Co. director	B	5–O	—	Bank chief clerk's asst.	£2,500
Clifford Gaunt	Post Office admin.	B	3–O	HNC, Municipal eng.	Building inspector	£2,500
Brian Gray	Docks foreman	D	3–O	2–A, HNC	Electrical technician	£2,650
Dennis Green	Tiling contractor	C	5–O, 1–A	1–O, 2–A, Surveying	Chartered surveyor	£2,250
Roy Greenslade	Insurance clerk	C	3–O	Journalism course	Journalist	£4,500

Name	Job		Education	Qualification	Occupation	Salary
Barry Hammond	Foundry manager	A	10–O, 3–A	Various, See pp. 92-3	Salesman	£4,000
Gordon Huntley	Plasterer	B	N/T*	2–O	Fireman	£2,600
Andrew Ireland	Transport foreman	D	1–O	Apprenticeship	Pipefitter/welder	£2,000
George Jackson	Police driver	B	4–O	—	Policeman	£2,500
Melvyn Johnson	Rail guard	C	3–O	—	Own business	£3,000
Jeff Jones	Pipefitter	A	4–O	—	Clerical work	£1,800
Gerry Kane	Brewery foreman	B	5–O	—	Finance analyst	£3,500
Christopher Kirk	Draughtsman	D	6–O	1–A, Inst. insurers	Insurance underwriter	£1,600
Howard Lane	Assembly liner	B	5–O	Chart. insurance	Insurance broker	£2,500
Paul Lee	Sales rep.	A	7–O, 3–A	B.A.(Econ.)	Trainee buyer	£1,650
Keith Lester	Electrician's mate	B	6–O	—	Fireman	£2,000
Derek Lever	Note **	B	N/T*	—	Trailer salesman	£2,300
Alistair Linton	Accountant	LD	5–O	Various accountancy	Management account.	£3,000
Neil Martin	Accountancy	B	7–O, 1–A	—	Stock jobber	£6,000
Rod Mason	Cabinet maker	A	5–O, 1–A	—	Control chemist	£2,300
Bill Miles	Proof reader	B	8–O, 3–A	Ph.D	Environ'tal researcher	£1,960
Gerry Miller	Ford assembly line	B	6–O	Elec. eng. Dip.	Signalling engineer	£2,700
David Millett	Ford supervisor	LLD	7–O, 3–A	M.A.(Econ.hist.)	Student/Some lecturing	Grant+
Tony Newton	Signwriter	A	6–O, 2–A	Accountancy	Develop. accountant	£3,250
Robert Parker	Crane driver	B	5–O	—	Stockbroker's asst.	£4,000
Roger Parry	Butcher	A	9–O, 3–A	B.Sc.	Research scientist	£2,325
Bill Pearson	Carpenter	D	2–O	Chart. shipbroker's	Shipping broker	£2,500
Alan Phillips	Ford sheet metal wkr.	A	8–O	2–A, accountancy	Ford accountant	£3,400
Ian Pierce	Ford semi-skilled	C	7–O	Studying B.Sc.	Student/welder	£2,900
Michael Potter	Stock controller	B	5–O	—	None	–

Continued over page

MEN

Name	Father's occupation	School Stream	School Exam Results	After-school education	Job 1973–74	Annual Salary 1974
Simon Reed	Note **	C	2–O	–	Commodity broker	£3,500
Danny Reynolds	Industrial eng.	C	3–O	–	Insurance clerk	£1,900
Jim Sanger	Office manager	D	7–O	Building trades	Quantity surveyor	£2,700
Timothy Simmons	Shipping manager	C	7–O, 2–A	Accountancy	Accountant	£2,000
Bernard South	Painter/decorator	C	4–O	City & Guilds	Electrician	£1,700
Patrick Taylor	Mayoral aide	D	Nil	1–O	Company director	£4,500+
Leslie Tisdall	Case maker	B	2–O	Failed 3–O	Cashier	£1,900
Gary Turner	Ford assembly line	D	3–O	Radio/TV servicing	Post Office engineer	£2,500
Thomas Ward	Shop manager	D	Nil	–	Transport manager	£3,000
Terry Warner	Ford manager	A	8–O, 2–A	Chart. accountancy	Accountant	£3,600
Peter Waters	Computer clerk	C	6–O, 1–A	Teacher's cert.	Teacher	£1,400
Geoffrey West	Steel mill foreman	D	Nil	1–O	Insurance clerk	£2,000
Mark Willis	Fork lift driver	C	2–O	2–O, Inst. of secs.	Accounts clerk	£2,000
Leslie Wood	Ford engineer	B	10–O, 1–A	–	Production engineer	£1,630
Nick Woods	Heating engineer	C	1–O	–	Asst. sales manager	£2,000

WOMEN

Name	Father's occupation	School Stream	School Exam Results	After-school education	Job 1973–74	Annual Salary 1974
Sheila Atkins	Tally clerk	C	3–O	–	None	–
Sally Bailey	Ford clerk	B	5–O	–	None	–
Sylvia Baker	Postman	D	5–O	–	Stock jobbing clerk	£1,400
Christine Barling	Docks welder	A	10–O, 3–A	–	None	–
Hazel Blackburn	Dustman	D	1–O	1–O, Nursing	None	–
Anne Bridge	Heating engineer	B	5–O	Shorthand/Typing	None	–
Susan Carter	Banker	B	4–O	1–O, Secretarial	Secretary	£1,400
Linda Croft	Milkman	D	Nil	2–O, Nursing	None	–
Maureen Crowe	Postman	C	3–O	–	None	–
Gillian Davidson	Electrician	C	5–O	Shorthand/Typing	Secretary	£1,700
Irene Davis	Rotary inspector	A	3–O	–	Part-time clerk	£750
Sandra Dean	Gardener	D	1–O	Shorthand/Typing	None	–
Jean Denning	Banquetting org.	LD	2–O	Commercial course	None	–
Marion Drake	Ford assembly line	A	7–O, 3–A	Education Dip.	Teacher	£1,400
Margaret Duxbury	Plasterer	D	1–O	–	Part-time shop asst.	£750
Mary East	Ford supervisor	A	6–O, 1–A	Commercial course	Secretary	£2,000
Brenda Ford	Ford assembly line	A	7–O	Typing/A-level study	Clerk	£1,400
Marion Fryer	W'house assembler	A	N/T*	–	Garage hand	£1,000
Diane Golding	Radio engineer	A	5–O	Drama course	Personal assistant	£1,680
Lynn Grange	Upholsterer	C	3–O	Typing	None	–
Norma Gregson	Ford assembly line	B	6–O	–	Office machine op.	£1,400

Continued over page

WOMEN

Name	Father's occupation	School Stream	School Exam Results	After-school education	Job 1973–74	Annual Salary 1974
Anita Grundy	Postman	C	5–O	–	Bank clerk	£1,800
Doreen Hall	Chargehand	A	5–O	–	Bank clerk	£2,000
Patricia Halliwell	Headmaster	LLD	6–O, 1–A	Teacher's cert.	Teacher	£1,569
Angela Harper	Fork lift driver	A	N/T*	4–O	None	–
Jean Hookway	Bricklayer	C	N/T*	–	None	–
Glenda James	Policeman	A	2–O	3–O, Commercial	None	–
Teresa Jenkins	Jig borer	B	7–O	Nursing/Commercial	None	–
Vivienne Kidd	Bookie's manager	A	7–O	Secretarial course	Secretary	£1,400
Julia Kilbey	Butcher/Security man	B	2–O	–	None	–
Janet King	Wheel inspector	D	Nil	–	None	–
Susan Kingley	Steel co. estimator	A	5–O, 1–A	–	Temporary clerical	63p hour
Jennifer Long	Driver	C	N/T*	–	Personal assistant	£1,500
Carol Longley	Baker	LLD	6–O, 2–A	Teacher's cert.	Teacher	£1,800
Joyce Marsh	Waiter	C	5–O	–	Clerk	£1,400
Eileen Matthews	Printing overseer	LD	7–O, 2–A	Education Dip.	Teacher/Market stall	Grant/ £1,000
Kathleen Mills	Ford printer	C	2–O	–	None	–
Angela Moore	Own business	A	8–O	Display/Retail course	Advertising exec.	£2,500
Evelyn Newman	Supermarket helper	C	8–O, 3–A	Occu. therapy	Occu. therapist	£1,500
Kay Norris	Ford stock handler	D	Nil	–	Clerk	£1,425
Patricia Pope	Docker	B	7–O, 2–A	–	Clerk	£1,500
Susan Pond	Juv. liasion officer	LLD	6–O, 2–A	Teacher's cert./Drama	Teacher	£1,500

Name	Father's Occupation		School Exam Results	After-School Education	Occupation	Salary
Sheila Procter	Glass worker	D	4–O	–	Clerk	£1,000
Cathy Richards	Coalman	A	7–O	1–A, Teacher's cert.	Teacher	£1,500
Judy Roe	Ford engineer	B	5–O	–	None	–
Janice Russell	Steel fixer	A	4–O	–	Clerk	£1,750
Valerie Sadler	None**	B	3–O	Commercial course	None	–
Alison Saunders	Timber driver	B	8–O, 5–A	Ph.d.	Cancer researcher	£2,089
Carol Short	Lithographer	C	4–O	1–O, Commercial	Secretary	£1,600
Pauline Slade	Train driver	B	N/T*	–	None	–
Carol Smith	Ford labourer	B	4–O	2–A	None	–
Helen Spicer	Ford assembly line	C	4–O	–	None	–
Barbara Squires	Fitter's mate	A	6–O	–	Cartographer	£1,800
Joyce Stewart	Ford foundryman	C	Nil	–	Shopkeeper	£3,300†
Hilary Street	Ford upholsterer	C	3–O	–	Factory librarian	£1,750
Ruth Strong	Lens grinder/Optician	A	6–O	1–A	None	–
Diane Thomas	Joiner	C	5–O	–	Bank tutor	£2,000
Joan Traynor	Crane driver	A	5–O	–	Shipping clerk	£1,410
Joan Tyson	Factory hand	C	3–O	–	None	–
Alice Watson	Wood machinist	B	3–O	–	Clerical work	£1,500
Lesley White	Toolmaker	B	3–O	–	Clerk	£1,500

Notes to chart

Most of the abbreviations used in the columns headed Father's Occupation and After-School Education are self-explanatory: i.e. eng. for engineer; org. organiser; Dip. Diploma; Chart. Chartered etc. One less obvious example: HNC. Higher National Certificate.

The School Exam Results column is straightforward: 3–O meaning three GCE Ordinary level passes and 3–A, three Advanced level passes.

* N/T stands for Not Taken, and refers to people who left aged 15 before sitting the GCE exams. 'Nil' appears for people who sat for GCEs without passing any.

** In these two cases both are the children of one-parent families, their fathers having died very early in childhood.

† The salary attributed to Joyce Stewart – £3,300 – is her estimate of what she and her husband *share* in takings from their shop.

The men

'I'm very money-minded. I need it (money) because I think I should end up living in a nice area ... I think a lot of the missus. Everyone does don't they.'

'I'm still uncertain about what I want to do, though I know I really want to work for myself and I keep coming up with mad ideas to go it alone. I will one day. I'm out for the best I can get.'

'I'm my own boss which I think is how it should be ... but what I want in the immediate future is some money to buy a house.'

'I'm a capitalist pig aren't I? I vote Tory. I've got to in my job, haven't I?'

———————

'When I go to the professor's house for drinks or a meal, I'm aware of my working class origins. I don't like the idea of putting on a false accent so I speak differently to the others round the table.'

'Like I say, you've got to play the game where I work. You've got to know when to push and when to be humble ... especially when you've got a background like mine.'

'I'm regarded as the traditional Cockney in my office, so I play up to it. All the others are public school types but they like me. I entertain them.'

———————

'Our social life is non-existent since we started a family. We go to see my wife's parents once a week and that's about it.'

'Where I live now is depressing, such an insular society. The people are friendly to our faces but that's all.'

'We don't go out much. There isn't anywhere close and even if there was I don't think we'd want to. How long ago was it since we went to the pictures? I just don't know.'

A selection of quotes chosen at random which set the tone to this section better than any I could have pieced together. Briefly let's start with the facts. Nearly every man – at the age of 26 – is earning more than his father did at his peak. The average wage for the 52 earners[2] is in excess of £2,500. (These are 1973/4 figures and would, of course, be comparatively higher now.) With that money they have bought cars and taken out mortgages on houses. They enjoy luxuries denied their parents, like dining out, holidays abroad, buying expensive furniture, filling drinks cabinets, and already in a few cases, considering the possibilities of offering their children a private education.

Since streaming played such an important part in their lives at school, it is interesting first to note the relation between school classification and present occupations and earnings levels.

Of the nine A streamers, four are earning more than £3,000 a year – three as accountants of various types and one as a salesman. Two more are in the £2,000 range, one as a chemist and the other describes himself as dealing with data control. Two earn a little over £1,500 – one as a trainee buyer and the other as a computer programmer. The ninth is still a student.

There are seventeen B streamers. Two earn more than £4,000 a year working in City stockbrokers, and another earns a little less as a financial analyst with Ford's. Seven have earnings around the £2,000 mark. These include the deputy manager of a department store, a policeman, a fireman, a salesman, an insurance broker, a local government building inspector, and a railways signalling engineer. (This last is indicative of the problem I discovered in adequately describing some of the more complex occupations. It is also a good example of the multiplicity of categories covered by the word 'engineer'. In this case the job is not manual and the man holds a degree.) Three earn about £2,000 – two of whom have Ph.D.s and are doing research. The third is a cashier. Two earn just over £1,500, one being a production engineer (this time a skilled manual job); and the second is an import clerk in a London office. The seventeenth is the only one of the sample who has no job – and who is not studying – and who lives, instead, what can best be described as a hippy existence.[3]

Of the fourteen C streamers, four earn more than £3,000 – one as a bookie, another as a commodity broker one as an accountant, and the fourth as a journalist. A fifth has just launched his own business and is uncertain about his earnings but he agreed that he is in the £3,000 bracket. Two earn £2,500 or more – one as a public health inspector, and the other working night shift on the assembly line of a car manufacturers while studying an open university course by day. Four are earning about £2,000. One is a certified accountant, another an accounts clerk, the third is an assistant sales manager and the other is an insurance broker's clerk. Of the remaining three, one is an electrician earning more than £1,500, about the same as the second, a policeman. The other man is a schoolteacher earning less than £1,500 a year.

There are twelve D streamers, two of whom earn more than £3,000, one as a grocer, and the other as a transport manager. A third man, about to take up the directorship of a shipping and forwarding firm, said his income was impossible to gauge but likely to exceed £4,000. Five earn £2,500 or more, and include a quantity surveyor, a shipbroker, a cost analyst, a telephone engineer, and an electronics technician. Three earn £2,000 or more, one being a bank clerk, the second an insurance broker's clerk and the other a pipefitter-welder. The twelfth gets under £2,000 as an insurance clerk.

The last two of the 54 are the 13-plus entrant, who is now a telephone engineer earning more than £1,500 a year, and the sixth form entrant who is an insurance claims supervisor earning about £2,000.

A number of important factors affecting the earnings of the group must be taken into account. Firstly, geographical location plays a major part in wages – a fireman in East Anglia, for instance, gets less than one in London. Secondly, there are 'perks' in some jobs which add to their financial worth. Some people have company cars, others have good expense accounts and one policeman, for example, lived in rent and rate-free accommodation. Thirdly, university graduates who went on to obtain a Ph.D., or men who finished degree courses only recently, are just starting out on their working careers and cannot yet be expected to be earning a great deal.

Certainly as far as earnings are concerned, there is no marked difference, on average, between the four streams. The margin between the top average, B, and the bottom, C, was a matter of £320. It is, however, possible to argue that the A and B streamers have, overall, jobs that carry more status, but the exceptions are so numerous that it is a very debatable point indeed. What is more worthwhile is to look behind the figures at the people themselves, firstly by sketching in the extremely important 'in-between' years which led up to the jobs they now hold. With the exception of graduates, men generally settled into an occupation after a number of false starts. Those with minimal qualifications started as office boys in the City, in insurance firms, with shipping agencies, banks and stockbrokers. Very few stayed long in their first jobs, and only three are now working for the firms they began with on leaving school. Naturally, those with more exam passes tended to obtain jobs with employers who were offering executive or professional opportunities and who were prepared to spend money on the necessary training. It is at this point that the lack of adequate careers advice becomes clear.

Keith Lester left at 16 with six O–levels and joined the Civil Service as a clerical officer. Prospects after two years did not look bright and so he moved on to a new office. In the next five years he had five similar jobs, each one bringing with it a growing sense of frustration. No employer, he said, bothered to utilise his academic talents to the full and he asked: 'What is the use of passing those exams?' Convinced that it was 'the office' that was wrong for him he took a job as a fireman, but when we met he was worried about the possibility of coming redundancy.

Nick Woods tried a number of jobs before 'settling down' as he put it. He began by becoming a shipping office clerk, but gave up after six months to be a trainee buyer. He was two years with that company but grew frustrated and joined a betting office as a settler. That lasted six months, as did his next job as a warehouse labourer. 'I had at that time a very real feeling of inadequacy,' he recalled. 'I couldn't seem to go any further down the scale.'

These two men left school uncertain about the direction they should take and, like many others, tended to drift until hitting something by chance. Nick Woods finally joined a factory as an office dogsbody and worked his way up to assistant sales manager. Steven Ayres, however, knew where he was going when he left school, aged 15, with the specific intention of taking up an apprenticeship in the printing industry. He grew bored after a year and stayed for another 12 months. At 17, with no qualifications, he ended up as a weekly visitor to the employment exchange, finally taking a London Transport course to be a booking office clerk. He gave that up too, feeling under no particular stress to do anything. On a whim he joined an import company as a clerk and stayed there.

Derek Lever also left school a year early and knew exactly where he was going, to work full-time at the grocery shop where he earned cash part-time at weekends. 'Money was more important than anything else in those days,' he said, 'and after 18 months a friend convinced me that I'd do better going into the leather trade making handbags and belts. It meant taking home £14 a week rather than £7 so I jumped at it.' A year later he decided on another change, this time working for a building firm. 'I loved the outdoors life,' he said, but after four years he was made redundant and spent three months on the dole. Derek was in no position to pick and choose and eventually accepted a job as roundsman with a soft drinks firm, another 18-month-long job. Now he is selling trailers – but said of his future: 'I'm thinking of having a change again. Basically, I don't know what I want.'

The fact that his search is continuing is untypical, but the search itself, for that indefinable 'job satisfaction', was very common. There were, of course, others with a singular target, like Jim Sanger, who left at 17 with seven O–levels, joined a building company under a studentship scheme to become a quantity surveyor. Then he was confronted with a remarkable sequence of events which began when his first firm went broke after two years. He transferred his indentures to another which collapsed 18 months later, forcing him to move again until he finished his course. He then joined what he considered to be an expanding firm only to see that go out of business inside six months, and he found himself, now qualified, on the dole. Happily he was not long out of work and is now with a more secure company. This exceptional catalogue was the worst of its kind I encountered but it was not entirely unique. A number of interviewees had suffered redundancy before the age of 26.

There were four people who did not follow the movement into offices, or at least if they did, they became disillusioned, and eventually ended up with more customary working class occupations. Notable among this small group is Andrew Ireland, at present finishing his apprenticeship as a pipefitter and welder. After working for one year as a clerk in two offices he spent six years scaffolding. 'I didn't like being shut in,' he said. The decision to take on a skilled job was made for financial, rather than status reasons. He said: 'I'm glad I made the move to pipefitting, I'm happier in this job than I've ever been.'

Gary Turner, now a telephone engineer, went straight from school to a skilled manual job. He says: 'I'm happy in my job using my hands. The people at the top have degrees and I accept that because I wasn't cut out for it.'

Bernard South was not so self-deprecatory. 'I'm good with my hands and I've got a bit up top too. At least, I have in comparison with the others at work.' He had been interested while at school in things electrical, and on leaving with four O–levels, joined a radio firm. He has changed companies since and he's now an electrician but he was quick to add: 'I'm a foreman and responsible for a department. I suppose that's only natural – me having a grammar school education.'

Leslie Wood's route to a similar position in the same industry was very different. He left school at 19 prepared to take a polytechnic course in physics sponsored by a company. But he failed the student apprenticeship examinations and is now in one of the production departments in a supervisory position. He said he thought he had failed to fulfil his youthful promise and was one of very few who inquired whether his earnings were much different from his contemporaries.

David Bacon's job as a bookie was more on working than middle class lines too, though his earnings were well above the four previously mentioned and among the highest overall. He had worked for a year in an insurance firm before joining a betting office. 'Best thing I ever did,' he said. 'I take home a good screw every week, never short for a bit to spend on booze at weekends. Office wallahs are mugs aren't they?'

These five are exceptions though, for the most significant move was away from the working class base. The single-minded approach of Melvyn Johnson – the only one of the 54 men to strike out on his own – embodies the essence of the movement towards new values. He had just made the break into his own business when we met and his progress to that point is an interesting example of the ladder-climbing many others are also attempting with similar aims – to be their own boss. Melvyn did not prosper at school but determined to work hard after leaving. He started in his first shipping firm as a messenger and rose to import clerk; he moved to another company as a more senior clerk and reached assistant managership before leaving again to become a manager. After nearly two years in that position – nine years in all – he gave up his employment to start his own shipping and forwarding business. His aim now? 'To build up my business and give financial security to my wife and child. Basically, I want to enjoy myself.'

The ideals of Melvyn Johnson – independence, security and happiness – are no different to those propounded by people who continued their formal education after leaving. Bill Miles is beginning his working career after six years at university in which he obtained a Ph.D. in marine biology. Now he has a job researching the food sources of the Brent geese in East Anglia, and the possible effects on these by the siting at Foulness in Essex of London's third airport. Bill works for the Department of the Environment but says: 'I'm my own boss in many ways, which I think is how it should be. I've worked my way to this point. I hope I'll always be involved in active research, but what I want in the immediate future is some money to buy a house.' He and his wife are living in a rented cottage because they have no capital as yet to purchase, unlike many of those who went straight from school to work. Bill's wages, at about £2,000 a year, are high considering it's his first job but low in comparison with many who started work nine years before him.

This situation worried Malcolm Dove, also in the early months of his first job after gaining a Ph.D. and earning £2,000. 'I feel conned by all that I was told. Why should I have spent all that time at university passing exam after exam, always under intense pressure, only to find it almost impossible to get a job let alone decent money?' Malcolm, who is working on a leukaemia research project, says: 'Less qualified people than me, like the dockers, get too much money.' Incidentally, he married one of his schoolday classmates, Alison Saunders, who also gained a Ph.D. and is doing cancer research.[4]

Three others – Kenneth Bird, Barry Hammond and Robin Edwards – did not complete their degree courses. Kenneth said: 'I went to Newcastle to take geology but I couldn't stand the work and I couldn't face any more exams. Instead I had a good time drinking and going out.' He failed his examinations and was sent down. Although university proved a bad experience he liked Newcastle and stayed to take a job, and eventually, to marry there. He is a computer programmer and says: 'I've no real ambition. I'm happily married and happy in my job. I expect we'll soon have a family.'

Robin Edwards also enjoyed the social side of college, but he said: 'I wasn't pushed so I didn't work and in the end I left.' After a couple of years at work, however, his yearning to get a degree returned and when we met he was again a student about to finish his degree in civil engineering.

Barry Hammond decided himself to leave Manchester University after his second year on an architectural course. He says his reasons for giving it up were that he knew he would fail and did not wish to waste his time. It was far from the end of his academic activity however. On leaving, he returned to the South and took a job as a supermarket group trainee, eventually becoming a senior manager. He continued to study and now has an amazingly diverse array of qualifications ranging from an external degree in business studies to an Institute of Grocers Diploma ... and from a London School of Journalism diploma to the Licensed Victuallers Association examinations. Now he is a salesman for a pen manufacturers and does freelance work as a market research interviewer. In both capacities he works alone and, like many others, said: 'What I appreciate is the feeling that I'm my own boss.'

This need to stand alone, to be answerable to no-one but oneself, was evident in nearly all my conversations with the men. Peter Waters, for instance, is a schoolteacher – the only one among the men – and yet said his ambition was not to be a headmaster but 'one day, perhaps, to run my own business.' He left school at 19, went to teachers' training college for three years and immediately took a post as a physical education teacher in a private school. In terms of money alone he is worse off than every other earner, but he lives deep in the West Country and says he feels the easy-paced life is ample compensation.

Three others – Paul Lee, Ian Pierce and Gerry Miller – decided late to pursue a degree. Paul spent two and a half years as an articled clerk in a bid to become a chartered accountant, but failed his exams because, he said, 'it was impossible to work at home.' Then he spent 18 months as a travelling rep, on building sites and in a factory before going to York University to study economics. He had left school with three A–levels and seven O's, so he had the necessary entrance qualifications. On leaving university, with a second class degree, he took a job as a rent collector and changed his name! He added his mother's maiden name and created a double-barrelled surname. 'I figured that employers would look down a list of second class graduates and my name would stick out a half inch more than the others so I'd get noticed at least. It was a bit of snobbery really.' Unperturbed by the fact that his ruse failed he finally found an opening and now he's a trainee buyer. 'I love the job. I've got the feeling that they're treating me as a bit of a whizz-kid.' He was one of only four who made a point of saying he wasn't chasing material wealth.

Ian Pierce, like Paul, is single. He is financing himself through an open university course in physics by working as a welder at a car factory. This situation was reached after years of frustration, brought about to some extent by over-confidence in his own ability, which makes him, he thinks, a difficult employee. He left school in the sixth form after a row with the headmaster and joined a local chemical firm. He was there for six years but rose to a point where he could go no further without the exam passes he did not have. He moved to a scientific instrument company but that lasted only a year 'because I got frustrated not being able to do things my way.' He became a barman for a year but could not escape his scientific bent and started his own electronics business. He says wryly: 'I ended up with debts of £500 – but I hope to do it again when I've got my degree.' Yet another who intends to be his own boss.

Gerry Miller did well at school, gaining six O–levels, but said he 'just did not desire an A–level course.' Instead he took odd jobs for a while, usually leaving after a couple of weeks, but once getting the sack for blowing up a boiler when making tea! He tried two jobs in insurance, then happened to read a booklet on railway signalling. So he, like his father, joined British Rail. He began as a tracer in the drawing office, took exams to become a draughtsman and was then entered on the students' training scheme, a five year course, three of which were spent at a college. He emerged with a degree-standard qualification in technical electronics engineering and now holds a junior executive post with British Rail in York. He says he enjoys his work but hopes to take an open university course in mathematics 'so that I can have teaching as a second string to my bow.'

Not that the graduates were the only ones to study. The seven who ended up in various branches of accountancy spent several years of learning, while others in specialist occupations like public health, electronics and building inspection also worked for career qualifications. Some men got bits and pieces of certificates and diplomas as they picked up and put down various jobs. But several never took an examination from the day they left school. Simon Reed was one:

'When I was at school I had this idea I wanted to get into the print but when I left I was 16 and then I found out I was one year too old to be an apprentice. No-one could help me, the youth employment office, no-one. They suggested that I should become a telex operator instead so that's what I did. I stayed with the Post Office for about two years, then I went to a commodity firm doing the same. I'd never heard of commodities until then, like most people I meet now. Anyway, I saw what was going on and I knew that it was better than being a telex operator. And so I edged my way into the office. Then just as I got moving a bit I got made redundant. In some ways that was good because I got this job as a commodity broker. There's good money in this game you know – and it's a right laugh in the office.'

The last sentence is important, for in a dozen words this man captures the essence of the feelings of many of his contemporaries. They are well off in terms of cash and happy about their general situation, looking forward to gradual promotion and steady rises. Although only 26 years old most appear to have attained their targets – security, marriage, a house, a car and a state of mind they called 'happiness'.

Bill Pearson, a shipbroker in the City, now living in Epsom, said this:

'I expect I'll stay in the same game and progress through the management ranks. I already have to entertain business acquaintants, and what with our friends as well, we have a pretty full social life. Looking to the future, I suppose we'll have kids when we can give them a reasonable standard of living.'

There is more than an air of contentment about Pearson's statement, for the final sentence has a touch of true irony. Considering his salary, his schoolteacher wife's salary added to the fact that they sold their first house along with neighbours to a property developer, thereby making a vast profit, he is financially secure.

In a very different, and less typical way, Leslie Tindall believes he has achieved a state of perfect and continued happiness. He also works in the City, as a cashier, and still lives in Dagenham with his parents. He says: 'Travel is what I work for. I set myself a target, then I save up for it and go. I've been everywhere now – all over Europe, including Russia, North America, Brazil. Now I have an ambition to go to the South Pacific. I'm saving.' So single-minded is Leslie that he works as barman by night to help collect enough cash to satisfy his hunger for faraway holidays. He adds: 'When I've done all I want to do perhaps I'll sit down and study. I'm so selfish that I don't think I'll marry. Anyway, I don't propose to think about that until I'm 30.'

Rod Mason and Raymond Crouch both live in country areas, and both have a yearning to enjoy, as they put it, the simpler things of life. Rod is a control chemist with a lifelong interest in wildlife –

'I've still got the tortoise I swapped for a sheath knife when I was seven' – and says now: 'I'm not the executive type.' Like so many others, however, after an initial struggle to find a steady job he raised a mortgage for a house, bought a car and now looks at his own colour television. A simple life – but secure.

Raymond Crouch is a village bobby – a police constable with no promotion ambitions who likes messing about in boats. 'I'm a contented man who leads an independent life. I like the outdoor life and I don't like routine. This job suits me fine. I'm my own boss.'

A familiar cry that, as we have seen, but it goes hand in hand with contentment in most people's view. Of course, not everyone was happy with their lot. Danny Reynolds, mentioned at the beginning of this section, believes he's got a raw deal. His problems of not owning his own home and having a dead-end job are obvious, but Patrick Taylor is on the brink of achieving what many would appreciate. He's about to be made director of a shipping and forwarding firm. He dabbles in stocks and shares and has a house in Bexleyheath, an area as far removed in style from Dagenham as could be possible. He said:

> 'Education doesn't come into it when you leave school. I left without passing one O–level and now I'm the boss's right hand man, sorting out all the problems. My father was one of six and he had a real struggle. He never earned much but he felt his job was important.' Now me, I'm a man of means with property and shares. But I'm not sure I've made the right choice. I'm not really certain I've taken the right direction. I'm beginning to ask myself more and more often: "Should I stay here?" And I don't know what else I want to do . . . except go round the world.'

Another unsettled in his job is John Douglas. He is an insurance claims adjuster, and says: 'I hope the future will be full of surprises. I'm still uncertain about what I want to do, though I know I really want to work for myself and I keep coming up with mad ideas to go it alone. I know I will one day. I'm out for the best I can get.'

This peevishness about a job, while unusual to the sample, is not, I suspect, an uncommon trait, and eventual aims of 'making it' remain similar whether happy or not with one's lot.

Only one man out of the 54, Michael Potter, challenged the overall system and, having analysed it for himself, lived on its fringes. His case, so different in tone from the rest, is dealt with in some detail in the following chapter.

We have seen how the working class boys have variously taken strides out of their former background. There can be no better illustration of this than to meet the group's highest earner, Neil Martin. After a couple of office jobs he joined a stock jobbers in the City, where after six years he's now a Member of the Stock Exchange and prospering. He says: 'It's a different world in that place. There, people spin a coin for fifty quid just for something to do.' His front as the sharp East End wise guy was not his only compromise. He readily accepted that concessions were necessary to maintain his job and further his career. His ambition? A directorship . . . 'and to earn a lot of bread.'

'A man may improve his occupational ranking by getting a job which requires greater skill, involves more control and carries with it a higher income without necessarily gaining in status vis-à-vis other status groups.' [6]

There can be little doubt that most of the men have assumed a status above that of their fathers in relation to their occupations. Quite naturally, therefore, their standard of living has risen in proportion. But what about the quality of their lives? What change in status has occurred in the rise from council house child to property owning adult? What has this achieving of a new status meant to these men? And how has their achievement been accepted by the more established middle class with whom they now associate?

Before I begin to answer these questions I must point out that seven of the 54 men have made no discernible effort to move away from their background and I shall discuss their situation later. The following remarks therefore apply to a group of 47. Thirty-seven of these are paying mortgages; three live in accommodation provided by employers; three live with their parents; one rents a cottage; one lives in a council house [7] and two single men rent flats. Thirty-seven are married and two more had, when we met, wedding dates set, having already negotiated the buying of homes. Among the other eight single men only one was 'courting', as he put it. No-one is divorced or separated. Ten are fathers, five having two children and the other five, one apiece. Despite these variations the life styles of the 47 are remarkably alike. In general, they are bound up in their personal problems, are interested only in the details of day-to-day

97

living and accept many of the social values and views held by the middle classes, whom they more closely resemble than their parents, but they still remain outside the middle class. They do not wish to be called middle class – and the middle class do not want them to do so. There are wide differences between their daily lives now and when they were young. They are, however, more happy to make comparisons with their parents' lives and their own, rather than their development from childhood to manhood. Robert Parker said: 'Irene and I live in a different world from our parents. They've never been out for a meal and they don't have people visiting for a sit-down meal, except at Christmas, and then it's a big performance. They've never been abroad either and they don't even want to go.'

Bill Pearson also thinks he and his parents are 'entirely opposite in their approach to life. I put it down to children,' he said. 'My parents had children early and in those days there weren't baby-sitters so they stayed in. It became a habit. My wife and I aren't planning to have any children yet, so we socialise – and that's becoming a habit we don't want to break.'

More than two thirds of the married men have no family, and many say they are waiting 'to enjoy ourselves first'. Their parents, generally speaking, had had children when in their early 20s. Donald Abbott said: 'My wife and I are more self-centred. We have the time and the money to have fun. Our parents did not.'

There was a recognition of the change in a woman's role. Many said, as Terry Warner, that 'my father was master of the house and my mother was happy with that. But my wife and I have a more equal relationship.' Not that the real meaning of equality is always understood. Leslie Wood said: 'Unlike my mother my wife's emancipated. We have a partnership and I'm not sure that I'm in charge.'

It is interesting to note how men met their wives. Most were introduced by friends or met at work, but pubs, parties and dancehalls were all mentioned along with the odd blind date, youth club and college. These meeting places were naturally used by girls from similar backgrounds, and it is therefore unsurprising that they have married working class women. More than half of these wives had attended secondary modern schools, the men showing a customary male working class leaning towards the wish to be intellectual superiors in their homes. It is also, perhaps, a sign of insecurity for in spite of upward mobility in their careers they are less sure of entering into close relationships with girls from the middle class. Two reasons predominate: firstly, a need to have a secure base on known territory, a wife with a similar working class background while stretching oneself at work; secondly, a tendency to gaucheness in the presence of a middle class girl, a person who might appear to have a sophistication, a worldliness, they lack themselves. Many men who mentioned 'equality', using their own relationships with their wives as examples, did so from a position of superiority. There was no real challenge, they considered, to their role as leader in the house and I felt that lip service was paid to a philosophy not truly held or understood. What is certainly true is that equality was rarely shown on my visits and a wife's role appeared to be a supporting one in the great majority of cases.

Leisure activities vary with parenthood or marriage. Eating and drinking are the most popular pastimes, whether married or single, and many visit friends at weekends and in the evenings. Visiting of parents and relatives is seen in nearly every case as an irregular event, and often merely out of duty. 'We see a lot of the wife's mother,' said Stewart Allen, 'but not much of mine even though she lives closer. I mean, I like my mother, but it's just that we don't see her much.'

Gary Turner said: 'We went to see our parents a lot when we first got married. It dropped off after a while. Now I think I see my parents three or four times a year, but Jenny goes over to see hers at least once a month.'

Money, it seems, goes straight to the stomach, for dining out in the evenings is the most favoured diversion. Steak, well done, with chips, is a frequent first choice. 'If we only nip in for an Indian we usually have a meal out on a Saturday,' said Melvyn Johnson.

Restaurant meals are the acquired habit of the mid-twenties, but in the process of growing up old habits have slipped away. Several enjoyed the cinema in their youth, now few go and none does so regularly.

Even the sporting activities which played so much part in their schooldays have been put aside. Only three now play football every weekend, and a handful have turned to games unheard of in the Dagenham streets, like squash and badminton. A couple also enjoy golf. Tony Newton still maintains a fanatical interest in cycling, pedalling to work each day and training every weekend. He says: 'It's difficult to understand why people who once played sport have given up ... I think they make themselves believe they want something else.' The former sporting stars now content themselves with watching others, from the comfort of an armchair, on television.

Television is part of everyone's life. More have colour sets than black and white, and only one, who is single, has no set. The television was often on when I called at houses, and on occasion was left switched on as a background to the interview. Many feel it is a bad influence but do little to avoid it, speaking about 'the box' as if it has a life all its own. The majority view was put by Brian Gray: 'It's on most nights but I don't take a lot of interest.'

Others said: 'Television's on too often.' Viewing habits were difficult to gauge. Most said they enjoy documentaries and current affairs, but on one occasion a wife, overhearing such an assertion by her husband, interrupted: 'Oh come on, you never miss Barlow or Morecambe and Wise whatever else is on.' Another, Colin Drew, said: 'I'd like to say that I enjoy the important things but the truth is that I get bored by discussions. TV is there for entertainment.' These latter remarks, taken in the context of people's political views and the rest of their cultural activities, give a truer picture of television habits.

Television's effect on people's lives is easier to estimate than their reading habits. About half the sample are library members, though four admit they do not use their tickets. And fourteen men said firmly that they never read books. Those that do read are keen on sicence fiction, historical fiction, 'light novels' and biographies. One or two said they read a great deal. Only six belong to book clubs and one, Richard Downside, was happy to reveal that he only joined because the books – a large selection of English classics in imitation leather – looked good on the shelves. 'I don't think I've ever read one of them,' he said.

Nearly everyone reads a newspaper of sorts during the course of a week, eleven leaving theirs until Sunday. Among the morning papers, the *Daily Mirror* is the most popular, followed by the *Daily Telegraph, The Sun* and *The Daily Mail*. On a Sunday, *The Sunday Times* has by far the most readers followed by the *Sunday Mirror, The Sunday People* and the *News of the World* respectively. A quarter of the sample reads two daily papers; and the same number, though not necessarily the same men, takes two Sundays. Only one has three dailies, and four have three Sundays. As in the case of television some are conscious that they do not subscribe to the 'correct' views.

Peter Waters, a teacher, said: 'I read *The Sun* at home for the sport and the sordid bits. In the staffroom, I read *The Times* for news.'

Magazine reading is not so widespread, many glancing at their wives' journals like *Woman's Own* and *Cosmopolitan*. Some say they have to read magazines involving their jobs, and others take journals to do with their interests and hobbies, like cars or winemaking. A couple subscribe to what one called 'nudie books'. Both are married.

Notably absent from the magazine list were political journals. The closest are *Punch* and *Private Eye,* each read by just three men.

I have already mentioned the fact that the cinema is not popular. The theatre is, if anything, still less popular. And apart from the odd one or two who are fond of music, like Barry Hammond and Bill Pearson, visits to concerts, the opera and the ballet are unthought of. Church-going was also unusual. Four only were regular churchgoers and five said they went rarely. All the rest do not go and most said they could not remember the last time they did. Christianity does not begin and end, however, with organised religion, for 21 claimed they believed in God. Fifteen said they were agnostic and nine, atheist. John Elliott defied classification, describing himself as a 'questioning mystic'.

If leisure does not consume a great deal of money how do these affluent young men spend their cash? Firstly, they have mortgages, or high rents, which stretch their budgets. Secondly, they have cars, usually new, saloon-type, high-powered vehicles. And thirdly, they indulge in taking holidays. Only five have never been abroad, and that not for lack of money but simply because they prefer British holidays. Of the 41 who have been abroad for holidays, 12 have been five times or more. The most popular country by far is Spain where 20 have been, some more than once. Very few have been much further than Europe, though North Africa is becoming attractive. Leslie Tindall is the champion traveller having been the only one to have consistently spent every holiday abroad. Holidays are an important feature of the yearly cycle. They are saved for, planned and enjoyed come what may. Historical locations and scenic beauty are rare reasons for making the trip. 'We only go for the sun,' said Mark Willis. 'We don't like the food much and some of the places we've been to have been really dirty. But you can't get that kind of sun here, can you?'

Some men have less time for leisure, concentrating their out-of-work spare hours on study. John Elliott, for instance, is still working away at a management diploma, having gained since he left school a whole string of examination passes in the field of accountancy. His ambition to succeed keeps him at his desk, but his movement into a rural middle class community in Kent ensures, he says, few neighbourly distractions. 'It's an insular society here,' he says. 'The people are friendly to our faces but that's all.' His eventual hope is to be a management consultant, a position which he felt might put him on a more equal footing with neighbours.

Barry Hammond's penchant for studying restricts his social life too. His life style is very different from the rest in other ways as well. Apart from working in the evenings as a market researcher – 'not for the cash but out of interest' – he writes poetry, some of which has been published, paints and has a fondness for opera and classical music. This range of intellectual activity was unique in the survey and I mention it to highlight the cultural barrenness of the others. Barry Hammond's pursuit of culture – 'My ambition is to be a very famous millionaire, but in an artistic way' – while an individual passion, is a very good example of the kind of working class thrust to achieve. He is still climbing, others have arrived on their chosen plateaux, but all are or have been scaling Class Mountain.

During my interviews with these men I found it impossible to prompt a discussion about politics. Most said they were not particularly interested in the subject and there was a notable coolness whenever I mentioned 'class'.

'It doesn't exist now, does it?' said Melvyn Johnson.

'It's such a pity to class people. I'm happy how I live,' said Patrick Taylor.

They were irritated by the word class and some, when confronted with it, seemed unable to grasp its meaning. Jim Sanger said: 'Class ended after the war. We don't really know about class differences in our generation. Look at me! I don't think I've suffered.'

It was very difficult to get anyone to talk in a general manner about politics. They were unwilling to discuss class and unions without relying almost wholly on anecdote, and when that substitution was outside their scope they turned instead to clichés culled from newspapers. Brian Gray said:

> 'I can only tell you about unions as far as Ford's is concerned
> . . . and they make me sick. I worked for a couple of months
> on the assembly line there and so I know. In the first week I
> was in trouble for working too fast. Well, not too fast, just
> working really. So the shop steward told me to slow down.
> And there was a lot of skiving. Anyway, another time there
> was a draught and the shop steward told us to stop work so
> we did . . . and I lost money that night. The next night the
> draught was still there but this guy had got nowhere with the
> management so instead of striking he came up with some idea

102

about having a sickness rota so that we took turns to have a night off. According to him the management would then see that the draught needed mending because it was making people ill . . . Unions stink you see.'

A common catchphrase on unions was: 'They were useful once but now they've got too powerful.'

Occasionally I pushed further on this point. Mark Willis explained: 'Well, I mean the unions were necessary before the war when workers got a bad deal and there were lots of people out of work, but now everyone's got a chance to get on. Take me for example. I mean, I've worked my way up myself haven't I?'

There were, in fact, twelve union members among this group, though in the main these were of the white-collar unions of NALGO and the ASTMS. None was active in their local branch and most belonged out of duty – 'because everyone else in the office is a member'. Richard Downside had recently joined the technical and supervisory section of the AUEW at Ford's. He said: 'Our whole office joined as a gesture after a couple of people were sacked. Like I say, you've got to play the game where I work. You've got to know when to push and when to be humble . . . especially when you come from a background like mine.'

The general consensus of opinion from these men was that class and the unions were enmeshed: working class people are members of trade unions. Beyond that few were keen to go. Middle class was not something they felt they were. They lack a class identity and, for want of a better phrase, are de-classed, walking in a limbo between the two, having left their working class parents yet not being accepted – nor indeed wishing to be accepted – by the established middle classes.

This fence-sitting is revealed in their political stance. About half the sample said they intended to vote for the Conservative Party at the next General Election, but about half of those said they would do so reluctantly, adding that they would rather vote for the Liberals, but did not wish to waste their vote. Eight plumped for the Labour Party, the party of their fathers, but the move was towards a moderate socialism. 'I think Labour must move towards the centre or another party will emerge,' said Terry Warner. Six favoured the Liberal Party. Two said they were floating, and the rest – a dozen or so – claimed they would not vote at all. Even among the committed voters there was an apathy towards politics, a feeling that whoever they vote for nothing will change. Listen to Alan Phillips:

'I've voted but I can't believe what politicians say. It's pointless to vote. Politics are unfair.'

Yet he is not approaching this problem from a revolutionary, or even liberal, standpoint. He went on:

'I'd like to see compromise between management and unions. I'm middle of the road.'

Keith Lester said: 'Vote? Never. What's in it for me? Nothing.'

For Rod Mason there was no dithering over choice. 'I voted Tory last time and I will the next. The Conservatives have big business on their side and they can withdraw support when Labour get in. I prefer government by the party with fewer obstacles.'

Looking beyond the next election, what route would they like to see the political path taking?

'Of course,' said George Jackson, 'Communism is perfect if it's done right, but nobody's ever done it right, so what we've got is best.'

Richard Downside said: 'I believe in the basis of Communism – but it couldn't possibly work.'

These replies embody the views of the majority. Discussion on alternative political systems rarely went beyond a quick dismissal, intoned with such weariness that it appeared as though it had been said a hundred times before and that it was impossible to add anything further. Others, like Thomas Ward, equated Communism with strikes and unions, and from that deduced that Communism must be bad. He said: 'The unions are trying to run the country and they're only doing that because most of them are Communist. Now that's not doing the country any good. I don't see how Communism can be good if all it's doing is making things bad for the people.'

The views of Mr Enoch Powell, the United Ulster Unionist MP for South Down, whose campaign for the Government to end the immigration of black people and to repatriate those who wish to leave, found passionate support. I noted a groundswell of racial feeling which I consider too important to overlook. It proved to be a subject upon which people had very definite feelings, though three did say they had not been confronted with the problem, had not given close thought to it, and therefore relied on newspapers to determine their views on Mr Powell. The majority were behind him – including people like Barry Hammond, a Labour voter. He said: 'Powell is marvellous. He's got a crystal clear brain. And he's right. We don't require blacks in this country.'

Peter Waters said: 'There must be restrictions on the blacks coming here. England is for Englishmen. We need a strong, white

English government.'

Apologists for Mr Powell were quick to point out that the Press had often distorted his speeches on race. His detractors thought the newspapers gave him too much publicity. A few had faced 'the colour problem' first hand, either at home or work. Geoffrey West said: 'My parents in Dagenham are the last white outpost in their road. Immigrants should go home.'

Gordon Huntley's next-door neighbour is an Asian doctor. He said: 'I've never spoken to him and I never will. I agree with Enoch. If I thought he'd become Prime Minister I'd vote Tory.'

Gerry Miller deals with black employees in his job. He said: 'I'm racially prejudiced. I have to bend over backwards at work to avoid saying what I think.'

Even among those who thought Mr Powell was too extreme there was intolerance. Keith Lester said: 'Enoch is wrong . . . but I can't stand Pakistanis.'

I attributed the remarks in the previous pages to 47 men, carefully leaving seven outside the main group. This is not because their life styles are very different, for as far as leisure and cultural pursuits are concerned, all but one live in a very similar manner to the others. But I did not feel it was right to include men whose attempts to move out of their former environment, or away from their working class origins, were stillborn. Neither could I include men who had fostered no aims of upward mobility whatsoever. In the former category are Jeff Jones, Danny Reynolds and Peter Adams; and in the latter, Michael Potter, Andrew Ireland, David Bacon and Derek Lever. Five still live in Dagenham – four in council houses and one with his parents. Bacon rents a bungalow in Essex. Potter is a drifter. Jones and Reynolds appear to have been victims of two separate sets of circumstances which have coincidentally joined to frustrate their Dagenham escape attempts. They did not settle quickly enough into jobs; and when they did they found themselves confronted by the mortgage spiral which neither, due to lack of capital and low income, could face. Jones had a good job in the office of an Ilford factory, cloaking it in a little mystique by saying that he could not discuss it because of the Official Secrets Act, and adding that he was on the verge of promotion. His career aim to become a business control systems manager, was similar in many respects to the ambitions of his aspiring contemporaries. He also talked with disdain of his neighbours in the flats. 'They'd turn any place into a slum,' he said. Peter Adams had stayed with his parents and moved from clerical job to accounts job to insurance agent's job, and more in between, without success. He is now a telephone engineer and says: 'I've never been happier.' He was about to marry soon after we met and was hoping to move into the house he was negotiating to buy in East London, the only man to move in towards the city. He said: 'I look forward to being an average family man.' Derek Lever's job movements also robbed him of mortgage hopes, but he is relatively content with his council house in Dagenham, showing no regret that others have moved away. He said: 'I prefer to see myself as working class. Up the ladder there's always a lot of backbiting. It's a rat race in the upper class.'

Andrew Ireland lives in a condemned house on the main arterial road into Dagenham, having chosen to take an apprenticeship in pipefitting at a late stage. 'I couldn't get a mortgage when I was a scaffolder and I can't get one now because it's bloody impossible for anyone earning less than £4,000.' He, his wife and child, are waiting to be rehoused by the council, but his future, he thought, looked rosy. 'Top men have worked at my level,' he said. 'I could end up as a managerial troubleshooter.'

David Bacon was another who stayed with his parents until he married, about a year ago. His job as a bookie is lucrative, but he says: 'I drink and gamble and never save any. Saving's for the mugs.' If he did get money for a mortgage he said he would not go house-hunting. 'I'd buy a pub,' he said.

There was a noticeably different attitude to the questions on politics with these men, a definite bias to the Left, with two prepared to vote for a Communist candidate. Two also said they never voted, and Derek Lever's cynicism was revealing: 'Everyone should take an interest, I know, but I was brought up to believe that politicians all line their own pockets.'

The Women

The women of this survey have suffered the same fate of all other women of their age and background in Britain today as regards their general education. In primary school they mixed with boys, competing with them at examination level. In many people's minds now, and more especially then, that was equality. The subtlety of difference, quite apart from that engendered in the home, was there

106

for all to see in the first reading books where father works and mother washes up. The stereotypes were developed in concert with their home circumstances and it would have taken an advanced social and political consciousness among working class parents in the mid-1950s to have seen through and fought against this propaganda. The variation in treatment between girls and boys extended to educational attainment where girls forced into passive, introvert, reactive roles often succeeded at examinations while 'boys were being boys'.

At secondary level, sexual discrimination is much harder to pin down. And at Dagenham County High, where nearly half the staff were women, there was certainly no conscious move to stifle the girls. There were no blatant attempts to divert girls away from academic pursuits, quite the reverse in fact, for the school was well aware that its standing depended on the number of people passing GCEs and, statistically, realised that girls did as well, if not better, than the boys. I therefore came to the conclusion that home circumstances played a far greater part in these girls' lives during and after they left school than the school itself. That does not mean that I have overlooked educational failings, nor indeed industry's and bureaucracy's failure to realise the wealth of educated female labour. But as we shall discover, this sample of girls were ruled by pervasive, personal forces of such a nature that any equality of education and opportunity would have been negated.

There were more girls than boys in the top stream at school, girls outstripped boys in the passing of GCE O–level examinations, and although fewer girls stayed on to do A–levels their results, on average, were better than the boys. But that success is history. Those girls are now women, working at jobs with lower wages than men, less responsibility than men, and duller prospects than their male counterparts – and that does not include the women whose 'job' is 'housewife'.

There are 58 women in this sample, 48 of whom are married and one is divorced. Among the nine who are single, one was about to marry when we met and one other lives with a man without having married. Twenty-nine are mothers, including one woman with four children and five with three. Twenty-one women describe themselves as housewives and one of those was out of work due to ill health. Therefore, 36 of the sample are working. One rather surprising fact emerges from the school streaming classification, which showed no link in relation to men's career structure, for the A stream girls appear to have fared better on average than their contemporaries in the lower classes. Only two of the 17 girls from the A stream are housewives, and four continue to work although they are mothers. This group includes five of the 13 in the upper earnings bracket. Looking at the B, C and D streams the incidence of motherhood and housewifery occurs in 50 per cent or more of the women in all three divisions. This A stream 'superiority' may simply be a coincidence or recognition of the school's selection powers. But since the school's streaming shows no such success among the boys, I have to confess that I cannot explain its female fortune-telling. In all other ways, the women who were once A class pupils resemble the rest of the women in the sample.

We have already seen one striking difference between the men and the women: nearly three times the number of women are mothers as men are fathers. Fatherhood, of course, is a relatively minor upheaval; motherhood keeps 21 women in their homes. Apart from that major distinguishing feature, among the women who work there is a vast difference in earnings between them and the men. The woman earning most has a salary of £2,000 a year, which is £500 below the average for the men. The women's average is £1,400.

There are also two distinct groups within the female earners – those who are following a career pattern, and those who are working as a necessity. The 'career girl' tag cannot, in this sample, be escaped, and includes three teachers,[8] an occupational therapist, a cancer researcher, a cartographer and a banking tutor. The other group is made up largely of women doing secretarial and clerical work. We are presented therefore with three divisions: 21 housewives, 30 workers and seven careerists. I propose to compare these groupings and then deal with them in turn.

———

Firstly, all 21 housewives have children, and apart from the one woman suffering from ill-health, I could discover no-one who gave up work for any reason other than pregnancy. Conversations with these women tended to be dominated by references to 'the family'. They were surrounded by infant playthings, and in most cases appeared reasonably content with their lot, though it must be remembered most had very young children and the situation was still novel. Very few questioned the fact that they had given up their jobs to have children, and there was general acceptance of a mother's role. Sally Bailey said: 'I want to be at home with my kids – just like my mum was with us.'

Maureen Crowe was quite emphatic: 'All I ever wanted to do from the first day I went to work was give it up. It's great being at home.'

Some of these women have forsaken well-paid jobs. A couple have left potential careers suspended in mid-air. Carol Smith was at college studying to be a nutritionist when she met the man she was later to marry. 'I gave it all up when I got married. All I wanted was a baby.'

Christine Barling left school at 18, with superb academic qualifications, prepared to enter university, but changed her mind about going so far away from home, and with some help from the school managed to transfer to a university nearer Dagenham. However, she decided at the last minute not to go at all, and stayed at the laboratory job which she had taken temporarily in the holidays. Two years later she left to do clerical work at a City insurance office. She met a man at work, got married and is now a housewife. 'I don't regret missing out on university, though I think I'd like to have been a teacher. We're planning another child, but when they're grown up I might see if I can go teaching.'

Following a poor examination showing at the end of the fifth form despite an A stream rating, Glenda James succeeded at college in recouping academic losses, and also learned to speak Spanish. This led to her taking a highly-prized job as a secretary-translator. But she became pregnant, gave in to pressure and married the father. Now she has three children and says: 'We are happy. It's all worked out fine. I have no regrets.'

She was one of five women who admitted that they married due to pregnancy, following pressures from home. Another, Julia Kilbey, said: 'I didn't want to marry and neither did my husband, but we were told we'd got to for our families' sakes and that was that. I suppose you could say we were forced to the altar by society.'

For the majority of the women in this section, however, there were no moral crises or political dilemmas when the time came to leave work. It was part of a natural progression . . . they left school, took clerical jobs and looked forward to the inevitable state of matrimony. Most did not wait very long either. On average, they had been married almost six years when I met them – just under four years after leaving school at 16. Of these 21 women, two left at the end of the fourth form, 18 left after the fifth, and just one, Christine Barling, took sixth form studies.

The working women group of 30 is more complex. Twenty-one of them are married and, on average, have been so for just over four years. The majority of them, 23, left school in the fifth form. Two left in the fourth and five in the sixth. Their reasons for working are diverse. Some are on the threshold of motherhood, if not in fact in spirit. Some wish to maintain independence from marriage, motherhood and life as a housewife at all costs, but have no particular career ambitions either. Five work in spite of having children, though not all for the same reasons.

Let's take a brief look at each of those three groups:

Susan Kingley, having picked up a handsome redundancy payment, is doing temporary clerical work in anticipation of 'starting a family'. The plans have been laid. Financial provision has been made. This planning is rather like that of Doreen Hall, who sees her future mapped out. With her wages as a bank clerk added to her transport manager husband's they are able to save a 'lot of money' every month. She said: 'We want kids so we're preparing to give them a good start.'

There is a certainty that there will be children. Joan Traynor, who said she felt she had taken many wrong occupational turnings after leaving school, accepts that her search must be interrupted. 'A family comes first now, and a career will come later.'

Janice Russell is one of many who said: 'My ambition is to have a family, and to see my husband do well, and to have a contented life.'

There are many who believe life will begin again after motherhood, meaning perhaps that life is suspended during the mothering, housewifely years. A number spoke of what they would do 'when the children are grown up'. From travel to teacher's training ... the dreams of the future make bearable the reality of the present.

Then there are the second group, those who wish to keep their independence, like Carol Short, who is still single and who claims to be avoiding marriage. 'I can't face being tied down,' she said, and looked forward to a period of Continental travel.

After leaving school Gillian Davidson took a year's secretarial course and has spent all the years since working for the same firm, gradually improving her secretarial status to the point where she now works 'for one of the partners'. She is single and hopes to remain so. 'I want complete independence to do as I please,' she said.

Although this is a common attitude among those who were single, one married woman wanted to make her position clear. Joyce Marsh, a Civil Service clerk, said: 'One thing I want you to know straight away – I'm not planning a family.'

The third group are those five married mothers who organise their family lives in order that they can go out to work. For three it is an economic necessity. Cathy Richards is a secondary school teacher in Devon, and says she would much rather stay at home to look after her 15-month-old son. But her husband earns little and she said she is willing to 'make the sacrifice' because they so much enjoy their rural existence. Their son goes to a baby-minder.

Another with a love of country life is Marion Fryer who lives in North Essex. In consequence her husband's wages are low so she works at a local garage, serving petrol and helping in the office. While she works her child goes to nursery school.

The more traditional working class baby-minder is 'mum', and Margaret Duxbury's two children spend the weekdays with their grandmother while she works in the accounts department of a local factory in Dagenham. 'We need the money,' said Margaret. 'Even with my mother helping out I can only work part-time, but the money's essential.'

Money, however, is only a peripheral reason for Angela Harper's decision to work. When we met, her son was six months old and she was training to be a beauty counsellor because 'it's the sort of job I can do even though I've got a child. I have to get out of this house.' When she became pregnant she had a top post in a foreign bank in the City. 'I was the first girl there to deal with the financing of foreign trade,' she said proudly.

The fifth working mother is Joyce Stewart who has three children. She and her husband live on the premises of a general store in Great Yarmouth, and are equally involved in its activities. But before they moved into the shop Joyce said her husband 'wouldn't let me work. He likes me at home.'

'Career girls' is, I admit, not the best description for the third major grouping, for there is no easy label to attach to the seven included under this umbrella. Some – like Evelyn Newman, Alison Saunders and Susan Pond – are fulfilled by the jobs they do. Others – like Diane Thomas and Barbara Squires – have won top positions by persistence and hard work.

Eileen Matthews and Marion Drake are in the throes of making up for past mistakes, plunging into teaching in an attempt to gain some sort of independence. They both had early marriages. In Marion's case this stopped her from going on to the expected further education. Instead, she had a baby and took a number of clerical jobs before, aged 22, she embarked on a three-year teachers' training course. Her mother looked after her child, as she does now, while Marion works at a local school.

Eileen had a sad beginning to adult life, falling pregnant while in the first year at teachers' training college. She married the father, despite parental offers of abortion, but after three and a half years the marriage broke down. Eileen, divorced, returned to her parents with her daughter and set out once more to become a teacher. She is now at college and her main aim is to win freedom from her parents. After years of disappointment and frustration she is determined to succeed. 'Security', she says, 'is my god.'

These two cases are very different from that of the only other mother among the seven, Evelyn Newman, an occupational therapist, who is able to take her baby to work with her every day. After three years at college and two jobs she is now head of a small department in a London dockland hospital, where a crèche is provided. It is a position she enjoys.

Like Evelyn, Alison Saunders has a job which combines academic knowledge with practical application. She is a cancer researcher. She has a Ph.D. in plant pathology and is the only woman from the year to get a university degree. This has not made her smug, rather the reverse, for she is consumed by the thought that the world is hurtling towards disaster. She is concerned with the protection of the environment, alarmed by the possibility of euthanasia and terrified by the subject of her own death.

Alison had an intellectual response to the questions I asked, and in a somewhat different way so did Susan Pond, a primary school teacher with some interesting ideas on education. Susan followed up three years of teacher's training with a 12-month drama course and taught English at secondary level for a short time before joining a primary school. Her ambition, she says, is to run her own school for maladjusted children.

All of which is far from the aims of Diane Thomas, who tutors the new recruits at a big City bank. She has steadily worked her way up from clerk, and she has the next step in focus too, aiming to move into the personnel department. This pursuit of money/power is unique among the working class female group.

The dissimilarities of daily life outlined in the previous section are also influenced, for those who are married, by their husbands. More than half the 21 housewives married men who had attended secondary modern schools. It was a slightly higher percentage for the 21 working wives. Only six women from either of these groups married grammar schoolboys. Yet among the seven married careerists, five chose grammar school leavers, while two married secondary modern boys.

The phrase 'a good marriage' for the women in this survey meant a love match with a boy from the same social background which might offer a stable and lasting relationship. It did not mean a marriage which afforded upward mobility. Only one woman, who is still single, said she was looking for a man with money and position.

Among the 42 married working women and housewives, 17 are married to manual workers, most of whom are skilled. A further ten are clerical staff. Three are married to policemen, and the rest have minor managerial posts. Two of the six 'married careerists' have husbands who are manual workers, while the other four include teachers and managerial staff. I ought also to mention the inter-marriages, that is the women who married men who had also been at County High. Four of them married men from our own year; one girl is married to a man one year her junior; and three girls chose husbands who were older. Sandra Dean's is the most fascinating story. She told how soon after leaving school she approached a man on Fenchurch Street station in London because she remembered him from schooldays. She said: 'Roger was my dinner table monitor when I was in the first form. He was in the fifth form, of course, and yet he was always kind to me – giving me extras and so on.[9] I remember saying to a friend then "I'm going to marry Roger", like kids do, you know. Anyway, he left school and I never saw him again until that day on the station. It must have been all of five years later but we hit it off right away. And that's how I came to be married to my table monitor.'

There has been a similar move towards private housing as shown among the men. However, it is the husbands who are the buyers in most cases, although a number of women stressed they were jointly buying their homes. Thirty-six women live in private accommodation; eight are in council housing; six are renting; two live in homes that go with jobs, one being a teacher and the other being married to a policeman. Seven continue to live with parents.

The difference in life style can now be seen clearly – between, say, the house-owning, careerist mother married to a teacher and the housewife in council accommodation whose husband works on the Ford's assembly line. But this is the widest of extremes. The structure is usually more complicated, and their own words do better to expose its complexities than the figures.

Linda Croft travelled by Green Line bus to school from the sprawling London County Council housing estate in Aveley, the sort of estate built in the middle of the countryside with inadequate transport facilities, little local employment even in the Ford's spare parts plant, and a problem of vandalism. It has no grammar school, the closest being a prestigious, endowed institution in Grays which took only the cream of 11-plus passes, and the estate's brighter pupils were encouraged to take up a technical education. For those, like Linda, who preferred a grammar school, it was necessary to travel. She did not do well at County High, leaving after five years without a GCE pass, and attributes this to the fact that her mother was very ill in her final year. However, Linda's mind was made up before she left school: she was going to be a nurse. She became at sixteen a cadet nurse in an Essex mental hospital and persevered with her GCE studies in the evening, eventually obtaining two passes. Her 18 months' experience on the mental hospital wards, though harrowing, did not deflect her from nursing, but she was poorly paid so she took a six month job in a factory before reaching the age of eighteen – and signing on at the Mile End Hospital in East London as a student nurse. She passed exams and worked hard but after 21 months she gave it up. 'The responsibility overawed me in the later stages. I was in charge of a ward, and I hated not having anyone to call on in an emergency. Once a patient died when I was on duty and the sister said it was all my fault. Although she was proved wrong the whole thing gave me the shakes. I couldn't stand it.'

This might appear to be an isolated case but it became a familiar theme for Linda. After a short time dental nursing, Linda took a clerical job in an employment exchange, rising over two years to a position of responsibility. Again it 'became too much for me. I didn't like the pressure.' In the meantime she had married and moved to Southampton, on to a council estate almost indistinguishable from the one at Aveley. She took a part-time clerical job until she had a baby, and when we met she had two children. She is a housewife, facing the problems of rising prices while her husband's coach-builder's wages are frozen, worrying about the effects of staying at home, hoping she might go out and earn again soon, dreaming of a pools win. 'I just want a temporary job,' she said. 'I'm thinking of learning to type. You can get a job anywhere then you know. But I don't want any responsibilities at work. I've got enough at home.'

She was candid about her position: 'I'm a typical in-the-rut housewife.' But she is aware also of what prolonged routine might mean: 'I'm worried I might turn into a cabbage. I've got to keep my brain in order.'

Linda's life is not untypical but, of course, it does not represent the majority as a comparison with another housewife, Teresa Jenkins, shows. She, too, left school at sixteen with an ambition to go into nursing. Teresa's father was a skilled manual worker and the family lived in a private house in Romford. On leaving school with seven O-levels she worked for a year as a shop assistant 'to get a break before my nursing course'. Her burning ambition to be a nurse was never realised for she gave up the course after a few months. 'I suddenly found I didn't want to do it after all.' Instead Teresa took a commercial course and ended up with a job as a statistician in a market research firm. It was an occupation she enjoyed. 'I know it sounds dull but it's amazing how interesting it was.' After marriage, to a bookmaker's manager from Dagenham, she changed offices and later moved out to Bedfordshire 'because of my husband's job'. At that point she had a child, and now has two. They are buying their house on a new estate and money does not appear to be scarce. In the evenings they rarely go out, 'perhaps to the odd party', except for the once-a-week routine when the local men go off to the pub while 'us women chatter'. They have an elaborate electronic baby alarm rigged up between neighbouring houses. Teresa is adamant that she won't increase the size of her family but is uncertain what she will do when the children grow up. 'I might tend to go in for commercial work,' she said, 'but as I say it's not very good having an ambition because it doesn't always work out.'

There appears to be little order to the lives of either Linda or Teresa, seemingly unworried by the catalogue of events which ended their schoolday dreams and content to compromise with daily reality, they are willing victims of life's vicissitudes. There were odd moments during some interviews when frustrations pierced the mask of apathy.

'I can't go through life with only two weeks holiday a year,' said Margaret Duxbury. 'I don't know how people can. I know I won't stand it.'

Even Sally Bailey, the woman who said she wanted to be at home with her child, said at one point: 'I know I'm vegetating being in this house.'

Many looked back and wished it had all been different. Diana Golding the teenager had pretensions of being an actress. Diana Golding, the 26-year-old woman, recollected sadly that her bid for the stage had been thwarted by a moment of shyness at an audition. She is now in charge of a typing pool in a local government office. 'I am in limbo ... just drifting. I always feel I could go back and try again but I couldn't face a second failure. I expect I'll get promotion if I stay in my present job.'

Joan Traynor was in a similar situation, having taken many turnings in an attempt to find a niche. 'I should have had a career,' she said, 'But I never had any encouragement to do so. I've drifted from job to job. Over the hill has always appeared greener. Basically, I think I moved hoping to find someone who would spur me but it hasn't worked out.'

Two others felt that although they had made mistakes in the past they were on the road to better things. Brenda Ford, whose school and home life had been full of sorrow, [10] went on into adult life without any sense of direction. She took clerical jobs in insurance for eight years. Marriage brought her a sensible and sympathetic husband and she spent five months working in a library during which time she realised that it wasn't too late to try again. Now she is back in an insurance office – but purely to earn a reasonable wage while studying for A-levels. She had arranged, when we met, a college course leading up to library college. 'I have been on the wrong road for nine years. I was scorned by my family for being the odd one out. Now I'm doing what I should always have done.'

Sheila Procter also had a disturbing home life, both parents dying before she was twelve, and she left school at sixteen with no particular hopes. After more than a year in a City insurance firm as a clerk she gave in her notice. 'I hated the anonymity of rush-hour travel to an office block where you saw the same faces every day.' For the next five years Sheila worked as a counter clerk in a small post office near her home in Ilford. 'It was the best job I've ever had but the money was hopeless and eventually I was forced to give it up.' Three jobs followed, all of which involved 'meeting people', before Sheila decided to write. 'I thought to myself I'm 26 and I haven't done anything so I'll try and write a novel, try and *do* something, something not everyone's doing. So I took a month off work and wrote. Of course, I had to get another job but I've written a lot now. And I think it's going pretty well.'

Women appeared to be much troubled by the problem of job satisfaction clashing with material reward. A number spoke of enjoying badly-paid occupations but turning in the end to more lucrative and more mundane jobs. Vivienne Kidd, for instance, trained as a secretary on leaving school, but discovered that her affable personality and interest in others led her away from offices into direct contact with people. For a year she answered problem letters at Reader's Digest. Later she was an employment agency interviewer, and more recently an estate agent negotiator. Now, however, Vivienne is saving to get married and is back working as a secretary. 'It's the only way I can earn decent money. I hate the job but the pay's good.' It is a situation she feels she could have avoided if she had had some career direction after leaving school. She said sadly: 'I regret the past ten years.'

For many married women personal fulfilment was secondary to making life more comfortable and more secure for their husbands. When I asked Irene Davis what she hoped for in the future, she replied: 'I just want to make Robert (her husband) happy.'

Janice Russell said her ambition was to 'have a family and see my husband do well.'

Even among those working women with well-paid or interesting occupations there are no promotion ambitions or ideas about what they might do in the future. There is no willingness to push themselves any further than their employers see fit. They are content with their achievements to date.

Patricia Halliwell, a teacher, said firmly: 'I've got no ambition. I like my job, but I wouldn't want any more pressure.'

Another teacher, Carol Longley, agreed and used a phrase I got to know well when interviewing women: 'I'm quite set here,' she said, 'I'm not an ambitious person.'

Mary East is single and still lives with her parents. She is a top flight secretary who moved from her first job because of lack of prospects. Two posts and five years later she enjoys the routine and says: 'I have no ambition now to do anything.'

Obviously the daily routine of a housewife differs from that of a working woman, but I was struck by the similarity of life for both during evenings and at weekends. The financial differences do not seem to be related to their mode of entertainment, which for the most part consists of pub and party-going. There are, as in the case of the men, the odd one or two who take an interest in music or the theatre. A few more said they were regular cinemagoers, but the great majority of them go only to see commercial films distributed on the main circuits. About a dozen said they still went dancing, a pastime in which nearly all took part during teenage years. Dining out is less popular than among their male peers, but the habit of 'visiting' – usually close relatives – is more pronounced. Lack of money prohibits some from engaging in a hectic social life. 'We don't go out a lot,' said Joan Traynor, 'because of the cash situation.' Others face the problem of obtaining cheap and reliable babysitters in private housing estates where nearly every mother has very young children.

Therefore the importance of television, particularly among the house-bound, has to be underlined. I was surprised to see how often the TV set was switched on in the afternoons, not as a source of information or even full-frontal entertainment, but more likely as a form of background, a sort of *vusak*. Among the variations in taste I did note a leaning towards drama series and comedy programmes. Women, on the whole, are less inclined to assume interest in documentary and current affairs programmes, admitting instead their addiction to the daily soap operas.

'I know it's not fashionable, not the thing to do and all that, but I like Crossroads and so I watch it,' said Maureen Crowe.

This kind of attitude, of apologising for doing or saying what might appear to be out of step with what are considered middle class values, is very common among housewives and noticeable too among some working women.

Like the men, married women have generally given up sport as a pastime. In contrast, some of the single women have branched out into new pursuits. Sylvia Baker says she spends as much time as possible riding horses; Jennifer Long and Gillian Davidson have a passion for badminton. The careerists are also interested in escaping from the home. Evelyn Newman belongs to an amateur drama group; Susan Pond enjoys playing folk music; Barbara Squires is a member of the National Film Theatre; and Diana Thomas and Marion Drake still play hockey. They also read more regularly and more widely than women from the other two groups, with the exceptions of Eileen Matthews and Marion Drake. Their press is, however, a strange mixture ranging from the *Daily Mirror* and *Daily Express* to *The Times* and *The Guardian*. On Sundays, *The Observer* and *The Sunday Times* are most popular.

Many of the 'working women' and 'housewives' said they do not read newspapers, and among those who do, local evening papers are the favourites. The *Daily Express,* the *Daily Mirror* and *The Sun* are the women's next most popular papers; and on Sundays, the *Sunday Mirror, News of the World* and *The Sunday Times* are the most common. Not that these newspapers are read from cover to cover, of course, and not always taken for their news content as Mary East's candid comment reveals: 'Well, I read the *Mirror* in the mornings on the way to work for the cartoons, and I take the

Standard in the evening for the horoscope.'

Again, like the men, women are not churchgoers. Fifty-one say they never go to church, though 25 of them did at some stage of their schooldays. Among those who do attend is Pauline Slade who lives in Italy after having married an Italian. She is a converted Roman Catholic. Joan Tyson is a member of the United Reformed Church having, she says, 'recently rediscovered religion'. She added: 'I'm really a Jesus freak now.'

Different again, and more typical, is Valerie Sadler's story. 'Between the ages of five and eleven I went to church four times every Sunday. When I went to County High my mother gave me a choice. I stopped right away. Now I'm an agnostic.'

If I had concentrated my attention only on the voting pattern of the women I might have recorded that their political leanings are decidedly Left. In comparison with the men this is true enough. Only six said they have voted Conservative in the past or will do so in the future. Ten more say that in the next election they will opt for a Liberal candidate. Nineteen said firmly that they are Labour supporters. That accounts for thirty-five, but what of the other twenty-three in the sample? Discounting the three living abroad, twelve women said they have never voted and are unlikely to break the habit and the other eight are certain that they will never vote again.

The figures convey so little, however, for the overall picture is niether one of political commitment nor political disillusionment. It is overwhelmingly of political naivete. Carol Longley, a teacher, said: 'Politics? No. That's for my husband to argue about. Mind you, I do have a special voting system myself. In the local elections I have no bias towards any party and at the other end of the scale, when it comes to general elections, I'm a swinging voter.'

Linda Croft, housewife, said: 'I can't say I'm well enough up on those sort of things to comment.'

I asked Judy Roe, a housewife who emigrated, whether she preferred the Australian political system. She wrote: 'It's all the same to me.'

Julia Kilbey, a housewife married to a policeman, said: 'I voted Labour last time and my husband voted Tory so I cancelled his vote out. No one can blame us for anything then, can they?'

These are very obvious examples of apolitical thought and are

119

representative of many such statements. The most common views are contradictory, prejudiced half-truths introducing opinions as facts, enshrining their attitudes in short, final sentences.

Diana Golding, a single woman working in local government, said: 'I believe there should be a redistribution of wealth. But the only trouble is that then the greedy people wouldn't work.'

Patricia Pope, a married woman working as a stockbroker's clerk, voiced a similar contradiction. 'I think every man has a right to withdraw his labour so I don't agree with the Bill.[11] Conservatism favours the few ... I don't believe in the Welfare State. It panders to those who won't help themselves.'

Carol Smith, a housewife, said: 'I am Labour but I like what the Tories do.'

And Sally Bailey, another housewife, recited the banal motto: 'Prices go up whoever gets in.' Her discussion stopped there.

The committed also deal in rounded, epigrammatic phrases that suggest a finality. For example, Conservative voter Susan Kingley said: 'I'm not ashamed to say I believe in every man for himself.'

Another Conservative, Eileen Matthews, said: 'It's making money that counts in this world.'

On the other side of the fence, Joyce Marsh said: 'I vote Labour. It's my background and tradition. Labour's better for the working class.'

Perhaps the most intriguing throwback to the past is Janet King's assertion that she always votes 'but I keep who for a secret – even from my husband.' Since she later said: 'I would like to see strong government cracking down on the unions,' I was under no illusion about her party allegiance.

Many women said they are 'anti-union' and one or two said, like Vivienne Kidd: 'I'm anti-strikes.'

There are twelve union members among the group including Hilary Street, who said: 'I joined the ASTMS even though I don't like unions because everyone else in the office did.'

Three of the six teachers are members of the National Union of Teachers and another left the same union because she disagreed with taking strike action. Patricia Halliwell is secretary of her local branch and says she believes in the need for strong unionism but added: 'I don't think I could ever go on strike again.'

At the time of the survey Joyce Marsh was involved in organising a strike by the Civil and Public Servants Association at the Dagenham Social Security office. She said: 'This is the first time I, or anyone else in the office for that matter, has struck. We need a wage rise ... ' Joyce faced stiff opposition from within her own ranks and said: 'I have more arguments with scabs than with management, but I don't feel awkward.'

It is noticeable that among those men who, out of choice or chance, have not made a move away from their class there are Communist sympathies. It is the same for such women. Maureen Crowe, a housewife still living in a Dagenham council house, said: 'The Labour Party have gone too far to the Right. I am pro-Communist and so is my husband. I believe in equal shares for all.'

Marion Drake, a married teacher living on the Becontree Estate, told how she was an 'avid Labour supporter' at school. She said: 'The party leaders have grown away from Hardie socialism. I wouldn't vote for them now. I'm waiting for someone to vote for. We need Communism — not the Russian Communism, but a proper Communist state where the people benefit.'

Susan Pond, a teacher, said she had once been a Communist Party member but left 'because although they said the right things they didn't do the right things.' She remains a Communist sympathiser.

I also detected the same measure of racial intolerance as among the men. A number of women said they thought black people ought to leave Britain. One, Norma Gregson, had spent some time living in South Africa before we met. She said: 'After living there I know Enoch's right . . . You don't see much apartheid in South Africa . . . I hope to go back soon.'

The catchphrase of the day is Women's Liberation, but I asked no specific question on the lines of: 'What do you think of Women's Lib?' Instead, I concentrated on getting women to talk about their lives, discovering if married women felt on equal terms with their husbands and finding out if single women were avoiding marriage. Again I have to resort to the contrasts evident in the three groups.

Among the 'housewives' there is an unquestioning obedience to the view that the husband, the breadwinner, is ruler in his own house. Of this group only Julia Kilbey spoke of freedom within marriage. She said: 'My husband and I run a sort of open house. We have a strange marriage to some people. I get as much time for fun as he does.'

The 'working women' who are married feel that going out to work is, in itself, a symbol of equality — a recognition of their right to share in the home since they provide part of the family budget. The inequality is shown when they arrive home from work to cook dinners and wash shirts. For the single working women, of whom there are nine, there is an enjoyment of independence. Four appear to hope for marriage eventually, and one lives with a man in a state of marriage – living incidentally in a style in no way dissimilar from the other married women. The other three are very happy with their single, unexploited lot.

The seven 'careerists' are much more aware of the need to end the traditional role of womenhood. Diane Thomas said: 'I am an individual – not "the wife".'

Susan Pond said: 'My husband and I believe in total freedom within marriage. We have a relationship which allows us both to follow our own paths whenever we wish. I couldn't live any other way.'

Marion Drake admits that she and her husband are 'growing apart'. Their early marriage had been a mistake. 'I live my life and he lives his. I have interests which he just can't share. I have freedom.'

Alison Saunders is not interested in seeing politics in party terms nor in reviewing her life with her husband in the context of 'a marriage'. She is too concerned that the world is unaware of its own death wish and says she lives in fear of the disaster. 'I don't want to die. I'm scared. Life is very unfair. I hate having been born.' Alison was the only women to discuss abstract ideas. Naturally her career at university, spanning about six years, has had an effect. She is far removed in spirit from almost all her contemporaries, and I can do no better than end this chapter with the words of Janice Russell, who unconsciously summed up the mainstream of thought for the overwhelming majority of women. 'If something doesn't affect *me* I have a negative view.'

Lonely Victims

In the course of interviewing so many people there were bound to be occasions when I would meet strange situations. Almost at the start of the study I discovered, for instance, that two women lived on opposite sides of a cul-de-sac in a new housing estate yet neither was conscious of their common past. I also found that two of the women who had emigrated to Australia both lived within thirty miles of Sydney, so I wrote informing them both. One replied: 'I *thought* that was Lesley who I saw in the theatre four years ago.'

Sometime later I spent an evening interviewing a woman and her husband. It was a friendly and open conversation, laced with such good humour that I was astonished by the reply to my final question, which asked what her hopes were for the future. 'Oh,' she said, 'I forgot to mention that we're in the throes of getting a divorce.'

These and other small, sometimes sad, sometimes amusing, incidents enlivened the survey, but they were nothing more than quirks in comparison with some meetings, which were too interesting to omit and which I felt should be recorded in full. Three people stood out. They did not fit into the general movements of social mobility and my interviews with them turned into lengthy conversations. On these occasions I realised I could not necessarily present a totally objective analysis of their lives in the context of class alone. The three people who provided this feeling did so for differing reasons. The only linking factor between them as children was that they all came from working class homes. Now all three are lonely victims of their backgrounds.

The first, Jean Hookway, was a friend of mine at school, and although we had not seen each other for more than eleven years, within minutes of our meeting we found ourselves able to talk in a friendly manner.

Michael Potter also remembered me, and it transpired that we agreed on many philosophical and political theories. I re-wrote the

123

piece on him three times before achieving what I hope is a fair reflection of his life and attitudes without undue bias on my part. The third person, Ruth Strong, was almost unknown to me at school – and the piece will explain why. This case was certainly outside the original terms of reference I had set myself. But I felt it to be of great interest.

None of them have much to do with the overall thesis of this book. They are presented here because I found them absorbing. I refuse to draw any conclusions from the three pieces individually or collectively. I also ought to add that they were not the only people among 122 that stood out, but they were the most helpful in regard to their 'difference'.

Jean Hookway

Jean was one of seven girls, 'one of those in the middle', and lived in a council house in a district just outside Dagenham, where the four-lane arterial road speeds heavy traffic from the docks at Tilbury past Ford's and on to London. The area is unkempt, with refuse littering the main road gutters. Even the grass on waste spaces is a dull green. The council houses are unappealing, designed like little boxes – solid, small and simple – with the accumulated dirt of three decades. Nearby, on the marshes, are unsightly factories. Always, there are the fumes from lorries and cars. I detect an ambience of apathy whenever I go there.

Jean's home, with four bedrooms, was bigger than most, but with nine people in the house it didn't appear large to her. She recollects that her younger years were fairly happy. Food appeared on the table at set times each day. Her mother was loving and jolly. There was little money left over from her bricklayer father's wages after essentials to buy luxuries. The hand-me-down world of large families, where toys and clothes have long lives, helped ease a tight budget. Anyway, other children in the street shared a similar style of living and she was unaware of missing anything.

Jean was a pretty girl with an impish smile and a cheeky character to match. She was given to laughing easily and even when angered you felt that a smile was never far away. She did not take life too seriously and no-one was more surprised than Jean when she passed the 11-plus examination. She later proved to be the only one of the seven to do so, and her parents were so pleased they found enough money to kit her out in uniform for County High. Like many borderline passes Jean found academic life at the grammar school tough. She said: 'I don't think I should have gone there. I just couldn't do the work. Of course, I was no angel. I think I clowned around in class as a front because I felt less intelligent than all the others.' Outside school Jean tended to remain with her old friends who had gone to the local secondary modern. She found their company far less demanding, and in the fashion of the times, developed an interest in motorcycles. More and more after school, when classmates would be bent over homework, Jean would swap her school uniform for the bike girl's uniform – leather jacket and tight skirt – to joke the evening away with the older boys who met near her house. She picked up the motorcycle gang's habits, their jargon and their anarchic attitudes. She was just fourteen when she fell for twenty-year-old motorbike-mad Brian.

By this time she had come to hate life at school. Despite being in the C stream – one above the bottom class – she felt that all the other children knew she was not up to grammar school standard. She resented teachers' lectures about her poor work rate, worried over her inability to understand a lot of the work, and enjoyed only the games periods, which freed her from the classroom, becoming very proficient at rounders and sprint hurdling. Jean was one month away from her fifteenth birthday when she discovered that she was pregnant. She recalls: 'I only went with Brian because I knew if I didn't he'd go with someone else. I liked him so much than I couldn't bear the thought of him with another girl. My mother gave me a book about menstruation when I was about thirteen so I showed it to other girls at school and they laughed. I did too, but I never knew why I laughed. My mum also told me not to go with boys – whatever that meant. She never did say why I shouldn't.'

Jean is not bitter. She speaks happily about the past, without prompting and without apportioning any blame, although later she did say: 'Brian should have known what would happen, shouldn't he? I certainly didn't enjoy the sex part. I just agreed to what Brian wanted, and it usually hurt me. Whenever I knew he was going to have me I always hoped that it wouldn't hurt this time. I thought a girl had to feel pain to have sex. I didn't have an orgasm or anything. I just used to lie there. I was very shocked when I got pregnant.'

Jean told her mother, who reacted with sympathy, and the school were informed. She says: 'The headmaster only worried that it wasn't one of his boys that had done it. There was no suggestion that I should go back to school. Anyway, I hated school so much I didn't want an abortion. I was glad to leave.' [1]

Jean was sent away to the country to stay with the local vicar's aunt. It was the family's first real contact with the church, and it was, perhaps, a little too sudden. Says Jean: 'This woman was too kind, always smiling and always near me, but making me feel odd. I felt so hemmed in that I ran away.' She entered an unmarried mothers' home in Surrey where all the girls were in the same predicament. From the way she describes it, the home had a naughty-girls-in-the-dormitory atmosphere, and because she was one of the youngest, she was treated well by the others. Her first baby, a boy, was born there. Meanwhile, the law had taken its course and Brian had been charged with unlawful sexual intercourse, for which he was put on probation for three years. When Jean returned home her mother treated the baby as her own. 'After seven girls,' says Jean, 'a boy seemed like the answer to a prayer.'

Jean worked for six months as a machine operator at Ford's and within a short time picked up her relationship with Brian. 'We used to go and see Brian's probation officer together,' she said. 'Funny that, isn't it?'

When Jean was sixteen she fell pregnant for the second time, and they decided it was time to get married.

Now she and Brian live in a council house in that same drab area where she was brought up. They have four children, and the eldest is now ten. Jean says: 'The older boy's beginning to ask questions — me being only fifteen years older and all. I'm worried about how to tell him. I regret it all sometimes, but then I'm glad to have got the kids over. It's turned out all right for me because I get on with Brian okay. Mind you, he's the guv'nor here. That's different from when I was a kid. Me mum was definitely in charge there.'

Brian is involved in the scrap metal business and his wage packet does not appear regularly each week. Money is obviously short. They do not have a car, though both would like one, and they rarely go out together in the evenings. She finds it difficult to afford meat. Their house is furnished sparsely and cheaply. Jean goes out one night a week — 'always a Wednesday' — usually to see friends, perhaps one of her sisters, and is still close to her family. She sees her mother once a week and phones her once a day. Pregnancy has stopped her from taking a job in the past, but now she occasionally works part time as a filing clerk.

Despite all this she faces the bleakness of her life with good humour and optimism. Wistfully she says: 'I would like to learn to type and to drive a car. I was always interested in nursing when I was at school, and I did once want to be a midwife. Maybe I will one day.'

Michael Potter

The day I met Michael he was on one of his infrequent visits to his parents. He was sitting alone in front of an electric fire, playing a battered guitar, drinking cheap red wine and, he said, composing a tune. Boozy, bearded and bare-footed, he was a stereotype of post-war, wandering, dissatisfied youth, from Kerouac's beatniks and on to the flowering cult of hippydom. His erratic and laconic style of speech was probably due to both the wine and the wariness acquired over months alone on the road.

Michael was an only child, born to elderly parents, and brought up in a tiny council house in the old part of Dagenham, near the football ground. His father worked on a building site, and his mother had a clerical job in the local Social Security office. They were both more than thirty years older than Michael. He says: 'I was isolated as soon as I was hatched. My parents were apathetic about me as a human being. It was such a sterile atmosphere at home. They just regarded me as a pet.'

This insularity became apparent at school. 'I appreciated the fundamental prestige of going to a grammar school from a working class background, but I seemed instilled with a latent rebellion. I just felt I had to piss about, but I could never work out why.' Without parental guidance, Michael had to find his own level and pursue his own philosophy. His irreverence for authority was obvious at school – 'I enjoyed discipline because it was a standard to rebel against' – and his detachment made close personal friendships impossible. He was tolerated at County High because he managed to water down his insouciance with humour, and because he did well enough academically, holding his place in the B stream by examination ability rather than continuous hard work.

He speaks now of the school's 'conditioning process', using the political term, but I felt he was more aware than anyone else during schooldays of the fact that we were part of the system. He stopped wearing uniform very early in school life, before it became fashionable to do so and not because of home poverty. One woman teacher did, however, influence Michael. She appealed to him he recalls, physically and intellectually, and when she expressed a personal interest in his future he listened. She told him to try for the GCE examinations, if nothing else, so he did belatedly, passing five without exerting himself a great deal. But he disliked the emphasis at school on academic and sporting competition. 'Why were we all competitors and not co-operators?' he asks. Then, as if to water down any significance the remark might have, adds: 'I guess we were in the transition period of progressive education. I suppose it wasn't too bad.'

The solitary schoolboy was not drawn into relationships with either sex. 'Of course I played with boys at school, but I never found one I could get on with. As for girls, I felt intimidated by them, although it didn't worry me.' Michael found, instead, that a guitar was more responsive and from sixteen he began to learn how to play. 'Funny how I hated music lessons at school and now I love music.' On leaving school, he took a job for a year with the Civil Service, moving to a local factory as a quality control inspector before becoming a timekeeper at Ford's. But that period of two years was used mainly to build up his musical ability. He helped form a beat group and they were booked for a summer season in Devon. It was the era of pop music, the time when four boys could band together, learn a few chords, buy amplifiers on the 'never-never', and blast a church hall into kingdom come. Small-time groups got bookings, and Michael's group found themselves travelling over England, and spreading the good beat in France, for two heady years. Then, in the manner of pop, the bubble burst and the group split up.

As Michael's friends neared the coming of age they decided it was time to get a regular job. Michael had other ideas. The pattern for the next five years was winter work for cash and summers spent on Devon coasts. He lived for a while with a girl but it didn't work out. Among the assorted collection of inarticulate and frustrated drop-outs he met in his summers on the beaches were that increasing band of university students who wanted to spread the gospel of their newly developed political consciences. He listened and says that he began to understand his background in a political context, and to question and to read. He was drawn to the works of Camus and Sartre, and a lot of what he said owed much to the French writers' existentialist theories. It was natural also that this life would lead to his experimenting with drugs.

The combination of confused political awakening, rejection of the society in which he lived, and over-use of drink and drugs created a period of nihilism. 'I got together with this guy one night and we began to talk about things. We drank a bit and swallowed God knows how many pills ... anyway I just said: "Let's get it over and done with." So we drove down to the beach and I hooked up a vacuum cleaner hosepipe to the exhaust. I turned on the engine and we took some more pills and lay back ready to die.' A policeman on routine patrol saved their lives and they were arrested. Michael was held in prison on remand. He said he refused to work in jail so he was kept in solitary confinement. 'I enjoyed that cell. It seemed to show that they were more worried than me.' He did not serve a sentence, and on his release by the court he turned his attention again to politics. He read Marx and Trotsky and, although refusing to join, attended meetings of a Trotskyist group. This growing interest in politics did not stop his guitar playing and in company with a friend 'from a mental hospital' he started to compose songs. 'We're a formidable team,' he enthuses mockingly, 'We're waiting for the call from Hughie Green.'

The mocking tone was one he assumed often in our conversation, deliberately attempting to smother the significance of any remark. When talking of political hopes, for example, he said: 'I would like to see the freedom of the individual in a protected socialist state.' But he qualified it by adding that he thought the position hopeless.

The mixture of flippancy and futility he generated was summed up in his final words: 'My only hope for the future is that I dematerialise painlessly.'

Ruth Strong

Ruth grew up on the Becontree Estate, but was very unlike the majority of Dagenham children, toughened in street games and urged to compete at home. In Ruth's house she was the 'ball' in a game in which her parents competed. The trouble stemmed from her conception before marriage, so hastening a wedding for which, perhaps, her mother was unprepared. According to Ruth, her mother resented her because of this and they argued a lot during her childhood. On the other hand, her father showed great love towards his daughter, which she reciprocated. Rows between her father – for whom this was a second marriage – and her mother were common. These would be blamed by the mother on Ruth and over the years their relationship grew more hostile. There were other problems for Ruth. Her father was Jewish and her mother Anglican Christian. They were also a poor family in contrast to the relative affluence of Dagenham neighbours. A major reason for this poverty lay in the fact that her father was disabled by an injury while working as a lens grinder. In middle age he made a unique and bold decision to become an optician. His years of study further lowered the family's standard of living.

Schooldays were not particularly happy for the painfully withdrawn Ruth. She did not join in with the other girls in playground pranks and was one of those who disliked sport, finding solace instead in solitary meditation and study. She claims that her Jewish parentage, and the fact that her parents could not afford a uniform, gave her a feeling of being second class. In spite of this detachment she felt her years at County High were good for her and eventually she did forge friendships, notably with two other girls from Jewish families. She explains: 'When I did make friends it was a case of joining the misfits. We were a group of about nine girls who didn't fit in terribly well. We were sophisticated, less noisy, less brash. We stuck close together and never ever mixed with boys. I was so nervous that I always got strung up when one of the others wasn't in the classroom. I suppose I had an inferiority complex.'

Outside school a Jewish girl friend introduced her to a Jewish youth club in Ilford, but she says she felt rejected 'because I was only half-Jewish'. She found the same lack of interest at the Methodist Church she later attempted to join. These experiences, linked in some measure with her not taking part in the school's 'religious lessons', hardened her attitude towards organised religion. She says now: 'I envy other people their religion. I am questioning but I dislike worship in groups.'

Quiet Ruth was a sensitive girl, again markedly different from most of her fellow pupils. Inspired by the idealism of a teacher who stayed for a few terms when she was aged fourteen, she joined the Campaign for Nuclear Disarmament. She also enjoyed poetry and revelled in her studies. She was placed in the A stream and gained six good passes at O–level. Although she never clashed with school authority due to her timidity she says she was inwardly critical of the teaching. She also dislikes the examination-cramming procedure in spite of having prospered under the system herself. It was no surprise that with her fine record of academic achievement over five years she should stay on for A–level study. However, she left after only three months in the sixth form, partly because of economic problems at home but mainly due to several of the 'Misfit Nine' having left in the summer. She says sadly: 'It was the biggest mistake of my life. I so wish I had stayed on at school. I wanted to study then and I want to study now. I'd love to read philosophy at university.'

Ruth became a junior clerk in a solicitor's office for three months, then did similar work for 18 months in the GLC housing department. Boredom and low pay drove her to take a job on the buses, as a conductress. 'My repressed extrovert side came out then. I always felt I was doing the job for cash and I overcame my shyness.' She needed the extra money because she had met a man at a dance and wanted to get married. He joined her for a while on the buses and after they got married they both went to college, leaving after just one year when finances ran out. In that short time Ruth got an A–level in English. She took a clerical job in an employment exchange for a year, and then worked in a share registration firm for another 18 months. 'Then,' she says, 'the trouble started.'

Trouble had, in fact, begun soon after the marriage when she suffered bouts of depression and felt unable to cope with daily routine. After several months her illness grew worse. She had hallucinations; developed phobias, mainly about travelling; and had a compulsion to check everything she did over and over again. Unable to maintain her job, she attempted suicide by taking an overdose. However, she called for help and underwent psycho-therapy for 18 months. Two more suicide bids – another overdose and a wrist slashing – followed, although on both occasions she felt compelled to call for help. At the time of my interview she had been having psychiatric treatment for five years, including a stay in hospital. These facts did not emerge until about an hour after the interview began. At first Ruth said simply: 'I've had problems with my health.'

Then she decided to discuss the problem in a little more detail. 'You must understand that I'm ill and the worst thing about my illness is not being able to explain it very well to someone else. I keep thinking I'm going to get better all the time ... The worst thing about it is the hallucinations. I had this idea that my father kept beating me when I was young – but that's totally untrue. He was so kind. I feel guilty about having such untrue fantasies about him. It isn't easy ... All I know is that I've got to overcome this health thing. When I tried to kill myself I meant it at the time, I really did, every time, but I always called for help immediately afterwards ... It's awful not having your health.'

Ruth's nervousness during our talk was apparent but she spoke of the future with some hope. Her 'health', she thought, was showing signs of improvement and she considered that her husband's placid nature had been a stabilising help in her recovery. He is now a part-qualified accountant. She cannot travel far because of a continuing phobia, she cannot read a book due to lack of concentration and she cannot work. She also drinks. 'We drink just about as much as we can afford,' she said. In spite of all this she talked knowledgeably about politics, current affairs and the arts. Most of her information is gleaned from magazines and newspapers, her only reading matter, and television. She said: 'Although I can't concentrate on anything as deep as studying at the moment I hope eventually to get more A–levels and get to university.'

Meanwhile, life for Ruth passes by in the confines of a rented flat in South London, although she considers that a great improvement on Dagenham which she called 'soulless and unimaginative'. She takes strength from her relationship with her husband. 'There was an intellectual gap between my parents but that certainly isn't true in my marriage. I know I'm going to be better soon. I just know I am. I've got to get over this.'

'Nasty Habits'

I disliked school dinners. Lunchtime would often find me in the fish and chip shop at Martins Corner. These visits may have helped ruin my stomach but they also provided an interesting insight into the everyday life of Dagenham. One regular customer was a woman who could have been anything between 35 and 50. She wore a headscarf, usually with curlers peeping out, and a black overcoat, summer or winter. A cigarette hung grimly to the corner of her mouth. She stood at the counter for hours, ostensibly talking to a friend who served the chips but in reality addressing the whole queue. Her voice was truly remarkable, pitched in the higher reaches and sounding like the screech of a power saw, it carried far beyond the shop across the road to the bus stop. When excited it went up an octave or two and closely resembled the whine of a jet coming in to land yet constantly overshooting the runway. My friends and I would spend hours attempting to mimic her shriek. To perfect impersonation you need genuine material and, as a gossip, she unknowingly obliged. I forget most of what Whining Winnie said. However, my memory has retained one marvellous monologue which went something like this:

'And do you know what? You'll never guess. Those people who live at the corner of Bushway, you know, the ones I told you about the other day. Well them. Well, you'd hardly credit it. Well, it's not so much 'im as 'er. I think he's okay really, but 'er, well I think she's running a bleedin' brothel. I do. I do really. I don't even like to 'ear myself say it. But it's true. You don't 'ave to take my word for it. Ask Elsie. She'll tell you the same. The goings-on since they moved in are no man's business. You've never seen the like. And 'er kids. 'Ave you seen 'em. Poor little mites. Shoved out the 'ouse wind and rain. Somefing ought to be done about it. If there's one thing I 'ate it's people with nasty 'abits.'

Even as a schoolboy I could see the irony of such a statement from this fag-smoking fish-wife, a woman who had seemingly cornered the market on nasty habits.

In this chapter I consider three subjects raised by the story of Winnie in relation to my 122 contemporaries. Firstly, speech and its effect on literacy; secondly, the use of drugs, including smoking and drinking; and finally, sexual attitudes.

Speech

The middle class children were aware that they spoke differently from the other pupils at County High. This difference went beyond accent. Their vocabulary was wider and their sentence construction was better developed. The middle class children, in homes with articulate parents, had grown up in an environment which stimulated more sophisticated speech patterns. It is not my intention, however, to compare the ten middle class with the 112 working class children in the context of speech and literacy, merely to point out that there was a difference and that we were aware of it.

There is a great temptation for people to label everyone who lives in Greater London as a Cockney. It is a mistake. In Dagenham and its surrounding areas there is a subtle mixture of the East London accent with that of Essex. The phraseology and intonations owe much to both and the result is monotonous, flat speech which has lost the sing-song spontaneity of its East London roots due to the unconscious grafting of an unattractive branch of Essex dialect. An article in the Barking Record said of the local accent that it was 'characterised by the sloppiness of pronunciation which, on occasions, makes it difficult to understand what the child is talking about at all. The mouth opens, tongue and teeth remain static, and what emerges resembles nothing so much as the plaintive mooing of an orphaned calf.' [1]

The residents of Dagenham, those who have grown up there, are aware of the deviation from East London speech. On any number of occasions I have heard Dagenham people describe someone as a 'proper Cockney'. The remark is a firm recognition that there is a difference, and is an example of the fine range of distinctions that exist among the working class who have left a traditional, settled urban area for an out-of-town estate. They wish to see themselves as having changed. The fluidity of the population creates a speech division in Dagenham between those — like Winnie — who retain some links with East London speech, and those who have attempted to pretty it up and derived what might be called a polite or respectful form. It is fair to say that this latter group, which is overwhelmingly female, is drawn from the working class with aspirations for their children. These were the bulk of the families I met when carrying out this study.

Three influences said to have changed working class speech are newspapers, the cinema and television. All have played their part, of course, and 'the telly' has probably proved the most pervasive of the media. But they have not had the far-reaching influence often attributed to them since it is impossible to substantiate the speech deviation that occurs among the sexes if media alone is responsible. The undeniable fact is that it is among women in working class homes that the erosion of traditional speech begins, and one agent that has been overlooked is the telephone. These machines are remarkable vocal catalysts. Many of the 'respectable' working class who achieved enough financial security were able in the fifties to have telephones installed in their homes.[2] They created alien situations for their working class users. Conversation previously had been a group activity, in shops, on street corners, among neighbours, with relatives. Confrontations with authority and bureaucracy were rare, though if necessary were carried out in twos and threes. I often witnessed scenes in the Becontree Estate housing office where one official would be dealing with a woman 'and my friend who lives next door'. Even if the neighbour did not speak she acted as moral support for the complainant.

The telephone changed all that. It brought the working class housewife into contact with the world outside and removed her from the group. She might once have used the abrupt form of speech endemic to her background – short sentences shrieked in strident tones. She would undoubtedly have demanded rather than questioned, and when dissatisfied with a reply would have repeated the same demand yet louder. In company with others she would be confident in herself. It was a 'them' and 'us' situation. But the telephone introduced a need for compromise in both accent and the form of address. A woman would soon realise that to get action by the person at the other end of the telephone would necessitate a softening of tone and the introduction of the same formal modes of expression. It was a one-to-one situation now. Without necessarily recognising the change herself she would begin to alter her voice on the telephone, to 'speak posher' as one husband termed it. It was a small step to the moment when she would use the same voice when faced with middle class accents outside the home. And a smaller step still to the time when her voice would change forever. In many cases the 'telephone voice' became the first sign of 'respectability' for, in time, the woman would realise she spoke differently from her neighbours . . and they would certainly notice before she did.

'Gives 'erself airs and graces, that one.'

'You're not kidding. 'Er Albert told my Fred 'es fed up wiv it.'

'Yeah. Bert doesn't change does 'e?'

Men confined to factory jobs would rarely adopt their wives' new way of talking. Working class men would leave the telephoning to their wives and were therefore less open to that method of change. They were also fiercely opposed to change in their daily habits. This, allied with the manly pride of being working class, produced subtle divisions within families.

I have already made reference to the mother's intense involvement with the education of her children, and there can be few areas in which she was so influential than in the refinement of her offspring's speech. How many hundreds of times did I hear a friend's mother say to him: 'You'll never get on if you speak like that. Don't say "ain't" say "isn't".'

My friend's reply that his father said 'ain't' so why shouldn't he, was met with the riposte: 'And look what good it's done him. You mark my words my boy. Speaking properly is the half of it.'

That sentence perfectly illustrates the speech problem. There was refinement without understanding. The mindless aphorisms of everyday speech continued in spite of picked up aitches. Sample just a few:—

'Life goes up an down . . . that's what I always say.'

'What's the use of complaining . . . life goes on.'

'Life's funny like that isn't it?'

Nonsensical end-phrases were also popular. 'Yer know' was inserted and added without reason throughout speech. Another common phrase was used as an exclamatory addition, usually after a comic story . . . 'ain't that real'. Apart from the use of these key phrases, gestures often took the place of speech. It was a simplistic method of communication, sometimes referred to by teachers as 'lazy speech'.

It was against this background that the pupils of Dagenham County High School learned their English language, and against which the staff had to fight. Research has shown that in one London working-class group syntactically simple language, which has been labelled 'restricted code', causes those brought up to *speak* this code to automatically *think* in the same uncomplicated way.[3] At the other extreme, among a middle class group, there was

136

a more sophisticated form of speech. Sentences were longer and more elaborate than those used by their working class opposites. This has been termed the 'elaborated code' and gives its speakers a chance to think in a more complex and abstract manner. I must add that these opposites emerged from studies at the extremes of the class divide, and between them lies a grey area.

Undoubtedly the working class Dagenham pupils were closer to the restricted code than the elaborated code. Attendance at a class discussion or a debate would harden that opinion. Therefore the County High pupils from working class homes were unlikely to express abstract ideas. Their mental development was stunted by their home environment.

Again, having set the background, I move on ten years to the time of my study. When I set out on this venture I had few clues about the problems I would confront. At the time trouble over communication was one I least expected to discover, although it was not long before I realised that it was going to have a major influence on my survey. People seemed unable to articulate their feelings and opinions on a wide range of subjects. In their frustration some would say: 'I can't find the right words this minute ...' Sentences would be left hanging in mid-air ... many would struggle for the right adjective and give up ... jokes and aphorisms would be chosen from an appropriate drawer in the mind to fill the void of complex thought. Personal anecdotes would be offered on many occasions to amplify a point of view, especially if I showed surprise at a reply. 'Well, I know that sounds strange coming from me ... I used to think that until the day I ...'

One incident in which a person had been involved was enough on occasion to change a point of view, and I discovered that opinions, once formed, were impossible to shake by rational argument. In fact, emotive response appeared to guide conversation more than logic. Hyperbole was commonplace – and a few wished their exaggerations to be taken literally. Opinions were offered as 'facts'. Argument was rarely confined to a subject for longer than a couple of minutes, to be replaced by an unrelated topic thrown up in the telling of an anecdote. All this occurred if I dared to question an attitude, which I did often, wishing not to argue but to clarify a point. There was sometimes an over-reaction to my question, a defensiveness perhaps, but more likely annoyance that the answer could be misunderstood. I learned to accept abrupt and vague answers, finding that attempts to clarify could make matters worse. I sought not to have 'don't knows' but the following example shows how I failed to avoid them.

One set of questions were connected with religion, the last of which asked: Do you think religious education was necessary at school? If the reply was: 'How do you mean?' I would ask if the interviewee remembered what form religious teaching took at school and whether that seemed a good or bad exercise. If the reply was 'It could have been better' I would then ask in what way it might have been better – by dealing with the New Testament, by having more discussions, by studying comparative religions, even by having no lesson at all. It was still possible to get a final 'I don't know really' at the end of what I considered helpful, if prodding questioning.

On the other hand, if I asked what the interviewee thought of Enoch Powell it was rare for a ready answer not to be forthcoming. Opinion had been formed by the media, possibly among the men at work, and in the case of women, often by their husbands.

Of course, the manner of answering questions was set by the person's attitude towards taking part in the survey, but as I have stressed elsewhere, very few were antagonistic. One man, Leslie Tisdall, rattled off answers at a steady rate and was obviously annoyed when I was still writing while he was waiting for the next question. About half-way through the interview I remarked on the speed of his answers. He said: 'I'm the sort that knows his own mind. I'm enjoying this a lot. It's not often that I get a chance to talk about myself.'

Most people, however, took the questionnaire in a leisurely fashion, and it was clear that not all 'knew their own mind'. Answers were sprinkled with the phrase 'you know', of which Fowler's Modern English Usage says it 'seems to be a compendious way of saying "I know I am expressing myself badly, but I am sure you are intelligent enough to grasp my meaning".' [4]

Most people have their own quirks of speech. One common over-use among many people I interviewed was the word 'basically'. For instance:–

'Basically yes, I agree, because . . . but basically, I'd have to say no.'

One of the most interesting specimens of exaggerated speech previously quoted is Neil Martin's:

'I'm a capitalist pig aren't I? I vote Tory. I've got to in my job haven't I?'

He was not the only person to add questions on to statements. I suspect that this speech pattern is Cockney in origin, though I cannot be sure. Whatever its roots it is a disconcerting habit for listeners who are inclined to find themselves nodding at the end of every sentence. It produces therefore the effect hoped for in a rhetorical question.

There was no discernible difference between the men and women in terms of sentence construction and content, but the assuming of a more 'respectable' accent occurred more often among the men. This is in direct contrast to the vocal change among the parental generation outlined at the beginning of this chapter. The need to conform in order to get on at the office, in mixing with men of a different social class, had led to a definite attempt at speech 'improvement'. One or two showed signs of gross affectation, but for most the change had been slight. Richard Downside was aware of his change: 'I guess you'd call it a classless accent,' he said.

About a third of the interviewees said they did not now read books. Derek Lever even claimed to have gone through school without finishing a book. He said: 'I can't say I've ever read one. I wish I belonged to a library because I'd like to know more . . . but I just never get around to it.'

The great majority of women at home read only magazines or newspapers. Among those people who do regularly read, 'light novels' are the most popular and that seems to cover everything from historical romance to thrillers and on to science fiction. 'What I mean by light stuff,' said Mark Willis, 'is the sort of book that you don't have to think about.'

It is no surprise that the relative absence of serious reading has resulted in a dearth of people engaging in writing. Three people spoke of their literary excursions.[5] John Douglas said he had once written a play but 'I had it rejected and gave up playwriting there and then.' Sheila Procter was concentrating all her spare time when we met on writing her novel. Her main ambition was to see the book in print. Barry Hammond, in contrast, was able to show me his work in print. A number of his poems had been published in an anthology, and he was writing more, along with short stories. He said: 'I enjoy writing, expressing myself, and I like to paint. But what I'd love to be able to do is write a symphony.' Barry said his reading 'runs through the whole gamut' and his book-lined room proved the point. His interest in writing was unique, although three post graduate students all mentioned a commitment to write 'in the future'.

Drink and drugs

Let me say at the outset that the word 'drugs' should in no way give rise to the thought that this group represents the drug-crazed generation of press fiction. Our schooldays occurred, for a start, a couple of years before the era of drug-orientated flower power imported from America's West Coast. Indigenous teenage tablet-swallowing was in its infancy. The point was well made by the woman who, in response to my question on whether she had taken drugs at school, said: 'People didn't have drugs in those days, did they?' No, the boys and girls of County High were busy instead inculcating themselves into the grown-up rituals of cigarette smoking and beer drinking.

A furtive group of boys would squeeze into a small gap between the bicycle sheds and the perimeter wire of the playground in a bid to discover nicotine nirvana. Some would go for long walks to the extremes of the playing field. Others, more bold, could be found in the pie and mash shop at the Merry Fiddlers. There was a great deal of huffing and puffing and coughing, but the most important aspect was to maintain secrecy. The school authorities frowned on smoking – several boys said they were caned for doing so, and one girl told how she was 'caught' with a cigarette by a teacher's wife while going home on the train and got a severe telling off at school along with the 'worst punishment possible at the time' . . . her parents were informed. Again, this stern attitude changed for the sixth-formers, and the boy prefects spoke of their room as if it was a smoking den.

Almost half the men said they started smoking during their schooldays while only a quarter of the women did so. Ten years later half the men and half the women in the sample are smokers. Very few who started the habit at school have given up. But the most surprising revelation was that about 40 per cent had never smoked a cigarette in their lives. Such people often accompanied their negative replies to my question with quotes like . . . 'and I'm proud of it' . . . 'it's such a dirty habit' . . . 'you'll never find an ashtray in this house.'

Few people could afford to be so self-righteous about drink. There are only three non-drinkers out of the 122, and two of those are abstainers for medical reasons. Sixteen did say, however, that they drank seldom or in moderation. I am not claiming that I uncovered a drink problem among this group, merely that drink plays an important part in their lives. Drinks cabinets were common; social drinking was one of the most notable leisure activities, and a few men spoke of the need to drink with clients during working hours. In many cases the youthful drinking of beer had been replaced by spirits. One of the signs of affluence was the installation in the home of a well-stocked bar.

'I wouldn't say I was a big drinker,' said Brian Gray, 'I might have a couple at lunchtime, and then I have one when I get home in the evening before my meal. Of course, if we go out I might have a few more. But that's not heavy drinking. You should see what some of the lads at work get through.'

The sentiment of that statement was fairly typical of the male viewpoint. Women would agree, but drank less. Their drinking, except for one or two at work, was generally confined to the odd evening and at weekends.

As I have said, drugs did not form part of the schoolday culture, but three people did claim to have taken some form of drug while at school. One boy said he once smoked cannabis, one girl said she took two purple hearts,[6] and another said she was prescribed sedatives by her doctor while in the sixth form. The first two both said they were not enamoured with their experiments and neither has since taken any drugs. The effect on the other girl of prescribed sedatives has been that she continues to feel the need for them and was, when we met, still receiving a prescribed dose. She had taken tablets through university on into post-graduate studies and now, while at work.

At the time of the survey, two other people – a man and a woman – were also undergoing prescribed medication. Both had done so for more than two years. Seven people – four men and three women – told me they had smoked cannabis in various forms. For five of them the one experience had been enough. One woman had gone on to try LSD, and continued to smoke cannabis. One man said he has also sampled a number of hallucinatory drugs, but he stressed that he had never touched 'the hard stuff'. he was still taking drugs but said he was not dependent on them.

To get the situation in the correct perspective I must end with David Bacon's reply when I asked if he had ever taken drugs. 'The only trips I've ever made were round Southend pier.'

Sexual attitudes

'I think mine was a gradual realisation ... I think the instincts you pick up when you're playing kiss-chase tell you what to do and when to try.'

'Sex shouldn't be taught in the classroom . . . and then again it isn't the parents' job. I mean, I don't think you should be that intimate with your mother and father.'

'My parents said they taught me all they knew, and knowing what I know now, that wasn't very much.'

'I learned all about it very early so I always seemed to know. But I still think sex education would have been a good idea. After all, some children don't have an Eddie Pemberton (one of his childhood friends) to tell them everything.'

These sentences betray the problems faced by parents in the transmitting of sexual knowledge to their children. Our generation grew up to find we had been no more than three years ahead of what was to be called the era of adolescent permissiveness. The fact that we were 'before' rather than 'after' is reflected not only in our parents' Victorian predisposition, but also in our own attitudes towards the sexual liberation which many of us believe has occurred since our childhood.

First I ought to explain what my questions attempted to elicit. My prime aim was to discover whether a formal sex education, which was not provided at County High, would have been beneficial and whether the ex-pupils thought themselves that it would have been a valid addition to their curriculum. Since the basis of this work is to try and capture a full picture of the former working class schoolchild I also wanted people to talk as much as possible on each subject. To achieve conversation in this instance I considered it appropriate to ask how they came upon their sexual knowledge and when their earliest sexual experiences had taken place. To formalise what 'an experience' was I also asked how old they were when they first had sexual intercourse. I concluded the section by asking about attitudes to the present sexual climate and about censorship. Some of these could be construed as intimate questions and they did present problems during some interviews. I did not feel sufficiently self-confident to ask every question every time, for instance when an interview was carried out in front of parents, as on one occasion with a man, and again when response to preceding questions indicated that I would receive undue hostility, as in the cases of two women. I was also less able to be specific in the questionnaires sent abroad – accounting for four more cases. However, of those 115 people who I did question as I planned only one woman refused to answer two questions. I think the relatively small number I failed to question may have important significance in relation to my own attitudes.

142

Sex was throughout many schoolboys' lives a predominant topic of conversation, and in a less obvious way it was prevalent among the girls. By that I mean that girls may have appeared to the boys as less absorbed by the subject but according to my conversations the girls merely managed to keep their interest more private. There were others, of course, for whom the mysteries of sex remained mysterious. They might have laughed at the jokes and smiled at the innuendoes but they laughed and smiled in concert with their wiser peers. They remained bemused. And if there are those who think I am exaggerating then consider the case of Doreen Hall, an intelligent A stream girl, who told me how she left school at sixteen without the slightest knowledge of the human reproductive process.

'I spent most of my last year at school giggling at dirty jokes and not understanding them although I think I got away with it. The others didn't know that I didn't know. But when I went to work the other girls in the office soon found out how green I was. Then the joke was always on me. I had a fear of sex – I just couldn't understand what all the fuss was about. My mum was too embarrassed to tell me, and because I'd laughed along with the girls at school *they* always thought I knew.'

Doreen was finally introduced to the subject, aged 20, by a sympathetic man who became her husband. 'I was so lucky Alan understood. He knew my mum was a puritan and he realised why I was ignorant. I'm sure others suffered like me.'

That assertion was undoubtedly true because other women told of parental hesitancy and their own shyness combining to delay their sexual understanding. Hilary Street said: 'My mother even got embarrassed explaining my periods.' For a couple of girls the myths began at this point as mothers avoided menstrual truth by indulging in magical euphemism. Sixty per cent of the men and 66 per cent of the women said they received no sexual instruction or information of any kind from their parents. And those figures do not include the parents whose only contribution to sex education was to leave around the house a medical manual opened at a convenient page. If this was so then just how did the boys and girls of County High discover the secret of life?

Many were unable to remember exactly, suggesting that they had gone through a gradual process of assimilation. One of the most common replies was: 'I suppose I just picked it up.' Word of mouth – in the playground, from older sisters at home, from older boys in the street – played its part. Keith Lester, for example, said his learning came from 'books and loose talk'. A number mentioned books as a main source, and one or two said they deduced from studying rabbits in biology lessons that humans did the same. But rabbits were saved for study until the fourth form – when pupils were aged 14 – and if a pupil decided not to take biology as a GCE course then he or she missed out on such lessons. Marion Fryer was one of those who gave it up and said she 'remained confused by all that flower reproduction' learned in the second form. A few said learning had simply been a matter of 'trial and error'.

Parents emerge in a strange light if what their children say is true. 'Mine simply gave me a doctor's leaflet on flies,' said Roger Parry.

George Jackson told how his father took him for a walk through the park. 'It was really embarrassing. I was fifteen and I knew all about it. All he did was stutter and I wanted to talk about football. I couldn't look him straight in the eye for days afterwards and I don't think he could me.'

The lack of a formal sex education at school and the failure of most parents to give positive help did leave children open to the possibility of wrong advice. There was a genuine search for alternative sources. Pupils found medical manuals uninspiring reading matter and turned to descriptive passages in fiction. Gordon Huntley remembered a week or so early in 1961 when he was befriended as never before by boys anxious to read his copy of D. H. Lawrence's *Lady Chatterley's Lover*.[7] His fame ended, he said, the day a teacher confiscated the book.

It was not the printed text that influenced so much as the spoken word – usually through the medium of what were known as 'dirty jokes'. The proliferation of such stories tended to trivialise sex, but they also may have helped boys and girls, robbed of other channels of knowledge, to understand, if nothing else, the basic mechanics. Only six people – four women and two men – said they remembered the jokes as being offensive, although many other women claimed that they could hardly be offended by something they did not then fully comprehend.

There is no indication either that those who took an early part in sexual play – familiarly known as heavy petting – had any different sex educational background to those who left such dallying until much later. Eleven women and 20 men claimed to have indulged in sexual play during their school years. Five women and two men also said they had sexual intercourse before leaving school – three of the girls as early as fourteen years old. None had any special parental advice, and one said she dearly wished she had, being forced to leave school because of pregnancy. This was the only case of schoolday pregnancy among the 70-odd girls of that year.

I asked no question on masturbation, but a couple of the men recalled that about half a dozen boys did gather during summer playtimes near the lockers by the physics lab for group masturbation. One man, Jeff Jones, said he was caught by a teacher while masturbating and smoking behind the bicycle sheds, and was caned.[8]

Against such a background of oppression, ignorance and misunderstanding it is not surprising that the great majority of the interviewees supported the view that some form of sex education should have been provided at school. They did so in the knowledge that it might have presented problems. 'Who would have taught it?' asked one. 'What age would have been best to teach it?' was a common query. Said Jeff Jones: 'Let's face it, by the second year it would have been superfluous.'

That does not appear to be true, however, for about sixty per cent of the group said they left school without understanding contraception. Marion Drake said: 'It's no good saying picking it up as you grow up is the best way of going about it because myths are passed on. We should have had films and talks on V.D. and contraception.'

She spoke as one who had reason to complain, being one of four women who told me they were pregnant before they married.[9] Three said they would have remained single if they had not become pregnant. One has since been divorced and another was contemplating a similar decision when we met. I also gained the impression that two other women had been pregnant brides. I mention this, not out of a wish to cast aspersions, but to illustrate the defensiveness of some women in these much-vaunted days of liberation when talking about sex. Significantly, not one man told me of a similar reason for marrying.

Among those who were against the idea of sex education at school were a number who considered it was the parents' duty to do the teaching. But the muddle-headed attitudes revealed in relation to other subjects came to the fore again. For example, Sandra Dean said: 'I'd definitely say no to sex education. It's the parents' responsibility.' She then added that her parents had taught her nothing.

Bill Miles said: 'Parents should make it clear that they can be asked – but they shouldn't necessarily tell.'

Rod Mason was also unsure: 'Sex education is a good thing, but overall I feel the less said the better.'

Yet another example of this kind of thinking can be found in the second quotation at the beginning of this section.

One problem was that I was asking people to make a retrospective judgement: Did they think sex education *would have been* useful? This led many to suggest that since they were fine upstanding examples of well-balanced human beings, who had overcome the problem of not having sex education themselves, then it had not really mattered one way or the other. Andrew Ireland put it this way: 'Sex lessons weren't for me then. But now they should give them as thoroughly as they can.'

Without any doubt the one comment that dominated all others in reply to the question over the possible benefits of sex education was: 'Well, not having it never did *me* any harm.' Very few people would admit that they had been troubled by lack of expert advice. Margaret Duxbury said she had 'distorted ideas', and Susan Kingley talked of being 'naive and inexperienced'. There was not, however, any evidence to show that people had suffered lasting scars, though my questions were not designed to investigate this problem in any depth.

For many people the first love has been their only love. Twenty-seven women and fourteen men said that they married the partners with whom they enjoyed their first sexual act, several of them adding that they delayed intercourse until after marriage. Six men and nine women waited until after the age of twenty-one before their first full sexual act; and three single people – one man and two women – said that they are still waiting.

These figures, along with those relating to schoolday sexual experience, indicate, perhaps, a slight movement towards growing permissiveness but no more. If the so-called 'sexual revolution' of the Sixties took place then most of the people of this age group were not among its vanguard. Their attitudes now towards censorship bear out this view. Cathy Richards said she would like to see the introduction of some form of censorship 'because things have gone a bit far now.'

Susan Carter said: 'Sex is debased if shown. There should be censorship.'

Linda Croft believes that 'lots of sex stirs up trouble,' but added: 'I enjoy sexy television programmes but I'm beginning to get worried about the effects on the kids.'

About half the men and women supported the view that a line had to be drawn, but there was little warmth for the Festival of Light campaigners. 'Mary Whitehouse has done marvels for pornography,' said Angela Harper. 'She's sold every porny book and film around by bringing them to everyone's attention.' [10]

146

Bill Miles, like many others, said: 'You can always turn the TV off after all. And you needn't go to the pictures.'

John Elliott was of a similar opinion but took a harder line. Although wary of giving whole-hearted support to Mrs Whitehouse he said: 'It's good to have those sort of people.'

However, Richard Downside best articulated the majority view. 'I like honesty but the problem is that you can get too filthy. When I was young I enjoyed the forbidden fruit. Now it isn't forbidden what is there to enjoy?'

Confessions were rare, but when offered were given in confidence. Four married women, for instance, spoke of having affairs. One man revealed that he had paid for two girls to have abortions in his late teenage years. 'I was on the rampage then,' he said. 'Now I've settled down, of course, but I was a real terror for sex at the time.'

Another man made it plain that he had had a long homosexual affair which he wished to discuss. He said: 'I did not share in the schoolboy sex bit. I was offended by dirty jokes because my parents were straight-laced. I liked them so I didn't like the jokes. I didn't like sport either so I didn't assert myself physically like other boys.' But he stressed that he is not unattracted to women. 'I am bisexual,' he said.

The re-telling of the tales of the growth of sexual awareness read like a fictional account of Victorian England. But they are stories only twelve or so years old and their subjects are either the parents of today or will be those of tomorrow. Among the men and women who are already parents I noted a definite bias against sexual liberation in entertainment or literature, whether it be the use of 'obscene language' on stage, the displaying of a naked body on film or the explicit description of sexual deviations in a book. There was a lack of distinction between the artistic and the pornographic. 'You can't justify any dirtiness,' said Clifford Gaunt. 'They all say it's art. But it's not – it's just dirty.'

That there was more than a measure of narrow-mindedness did not prevent people from favourably comparing their values with those of their parents' generation. Almost all considered that the situation had improved since their parents were children – though in what way some were less sure. 'My parents had a really puritan upbringing,' said Bernard South. 'They were very shocked if something a bid dodgy came on the telly – a passionate kiss or what-have-you. Then I felt embarrassed because they did.' Like so many others he believed sex education outside the home would have been less traumatic than his delayed and mystical realisation of the truth. He added: 'Sex education is a good idea but we still must have censorship to stop the dirtiness creeping in.'

The belief that 'things have got a lot better nowadays,' as a number of men and women said, was often belied by the kind of prudishness displayed in this remark by Joyce Marsh. 'If sex education leads to talking about it like this then I don't agree with it.'

PART THREE

In Conclusion

The Domesticated Class

I must preface this final chapter by recording that I do not wish
readers to believe that I set out to denigrate my contemporaries. I
also do not wish the people who took part in the study to think that
I inveigled my way into their homes, and to share in their
confidences, to exploit them for my own personal gain or
amusement. I took no pleasure in putting together some of the
sections in this book and I spent many a weekend, after a
week-long series of interviews, with a feeling of sadness. I had been
prepared to find that my friends had spent their after-school years,
like me, chasing material reward and managerial power. I expected
to visit lots of privately-owned houses with expensive electrical
gimmickry. I knew that most people would have entered a world
different in style and emphasis from their working class
backgrounds. Nevertheless I was unprepared for my major
discovery, that my generation had taken the narrow path to apathy
and complacency. I would never have guessed that they would
become totally passive consumers devoured and digested so easily
by the system. Instead of maturing and progressing over the ten
years since leaving school they appeared to have lost any
individuality and rebelliousness of spirit. Incurious, inarticulate,
almost inanimate they are the quintessence of quiescence. For
them, life is not so much a mystery, more a non-event. Some who
dared to look over the hedge in search of other roads were unable
to comprehend and fled back to the safety of the well-trodden
route. Just one or two who strode out down avenues of light have
been rewarded with open and inquiring minds.

I could not, however, feel antagonistic towards the men and
women whose lives make up this depressing dossier. They were
never provided with a map enabling them to discover new roads on
the route to freedom of thought. My anger is reserved for the
system — political, economic and educational — which enjoys its
perpetuation due to the operation of such a cynical, almost clinical,
method of indoctrination. I make this assertion not wildly or

151

without thought, for how can I believe otherwise when I see first-hand the results of Britain's much-vaunted democratic, free and open education system? And this in a grammar school, symbol of the competitive and elitist principle favoured by the ruling classes for working class advancement.

When I began this study I was not blinkered by theories. My questions were designed not to trap but to discover what made people tick. I wanted to know how people had progressed, digressed and transgressed, and what they thought about themselves. If what I have written makes any one of them bitter then I will be pleased only if that person profits from the acrimony by asking questions of himself. A re-examination is the only way of changing oneself. After asking questions of oneself the next logical step is to ask questions of the system. Although I would hope for this book to act as a catalyst for its characters I fear that it will be received by them with the indifference bred by a system which survives on the relative apathy of its servants. I did not write this book however merely to save one group of people from delusionary degradation but to assault the consciences of all who support it, either in ignorance or in despair.

Whenever distinctions are made it is natural that people allocated positions of inferiority will resent others being granted superiority. Schoolchildren in Britain are forced into this system of top and bottom, winner and loser. They are urged to compete with each other for their own good. They learn over the years of schooling that competition is not merely an honourable way of life, but the only way of life. The boys and girls who reached County High knew the score. At their junior schools they had been coached to pass the 11-plus after, in many cases, being streamed into top classes. On passing they left behind scores of their friends, the people who they had grown up with in the streets. While their mates went off to the secondary modern they joined with the selected groups from other schools at County High. Within a year the selection of the selected took place when they were streamed. One whole class was alienated – the D stream; many of the C stream resented their position; and some of the B pupils were annoyed at not being considered as A material. No amount of explanation on the lines of 'placed in the best class to suit personality and thus gain the maximum from the individual child' holds water. Once a pupil feels the school has dealt out rough justice he finds it difficult to maintain any interest in education. Banks and Finlayson discovered in their study among boys at three different types of secondary school that 'a boy who does badly academically is predisposed to reject the system which has placed him in an inferior position, and in extreme conditions an anti-school culture may develop. Successful boys are predisposed to accept the school's culture.' [1]

There was a feeling among the D-stream pupils that they were outcasts, tolerated by necessity. Within the class over the years between second and fifth forms a definite 'anti-school culture' developed. Some of the pupils keenly felt this rejection, and in spite of early attempts to overcome it, were sucked into the vacuum. On hindsight one remarked: 'The D-stream scruffs pulled me down.' Nearly all felt this same inescapable collective identity with the 'bottom' class. This self-image changed when they went out to work, gaining equal status with other school leavers in the eyes of their employers. Materially, most of the men are doing as well as the others. The lasting mark is a tendency among nearly all former D-streamers to be cynical.

There were also several streaming anomalies which added weight to the argument against. But the school considered that all kinks in the streaming system were ironed out in the fourth form by cross-streaming in individual subjects. This only led to complaints about that kind of streaming as well. And one is entitled to ask: If the effects of streaming were supposed to be minimised by the cross-streaming method was that not an admittance by school authorities that they were aware of streaming problems?

Streaming, a process for creating 'worthwhile' and 'worthless' sections, gave part of the intake the chance that was supposed to be open to all. It set a ceiling on many children's aspirations and expectations, though streaming does not seem to have resulted in adult life in the wide differences evident at school. The school lumped together its D-stream pupils with a cynical disregard for their future and gave them what it believed was its second class education. Certainly the D-streamers' final examination results were not as good as those of the other three streams, but the fact that nearly all have now become almost indistinguishable from their more fortunate contemporaries confirms my view that the first class education was designed only for examination training.

This takes us on to a further stress which caused disaffection – the pressure of exams. For exams at County High, even if certain teachers admitted a personal distaste for them, were the only yardstick of academic ability. Some able pupils found the exam strain unbearable. It is obvious that examinations test a pupil's skill at passing them, no more. Research has shown that some people's personalities adjust better to examinations and the need for revision than others. Introverts, for example, do better on the whole than extroverts. Exams are therefore a divisive measure if used without reference to the individual pupil.

I could overstate the problems I encountered in regard to home background and its effects on academic performance because the middle class sample was so small in relation to the working class sample. Firm conclusions cannot be drawn when comparing ten people with one hundred and twelve. It is however significant that none of the seven children from middle class homes who began at County High aged eleven landed up in the D stream, and none of them were among the fourth form leavers. With one exception they did not find it easy to adjust to their classmates but this did not hinder their academic achievements. It is interesting to speculate if the reverse situation had occurred on the fate of ten working class children in a school populated by middle class. Would they have prospered in spite of adjustment problems?

Having briefly considered three of the divisive forces at work in County High – streaming, exams and status – I want to widen the argument. I condemn those divisions but I also understand that they are an inevitability of schooling based on competition. Yet they alone do not explain the kind of adults who have emerged from County High, for they are just the mechanics of a sinister system.

County High, like every State school, was influenced by one undeniable pressure – the nation's economic need. Once the political Establishment sets its economic course it gears its education system to meet the work force requirements. Grammar schools were once seen as the best conveyor belt to produce sufficient trained manpower for an expansionist economy. Industry demanded then, as now, a skilled and educated labour force during a period of increasingly complex technological progress. I do not wish to argue about the education system's success or failure in the field of providing the right balance of multi-skilled labour and management over the past twenty years, merely to record the effort as a fact. This economic pressure has led the educational apparatus to make its greatest single contribution to the political system of Britain, namely the transmission, perhaps unconsciously but very convincingly, of the values and merits of capitalism. By that I mean that children are trained to believe that the economy should make individuals wealthier.[2] Wealth becomes synonymous with success. Therefore at school the pupils learn that they must work hard to pass exams to get a good job to achieve wealth – and, in turn, wealth will provide them with a new status in society. In simple

154

form they learn the capitalist dynamic: cash, with dividends and profits, provides incentive for hard work, thrift, initiative, ambition, self-reliance and self-interest. (Traits incidentally which are the hallmark of the British middle class.) Play a full part in the consumer society to pass through the gateway to a good life. In short, money talks. Why don't you make it talk for you?

It is not an exaggeration to say that County High pupils were eager recipients of such propaganda. The majority of them were keen to achieve a 'higher' status . . . and the justification for making money was most acceptable.

Maybe all this is a truism. No one expects schools to do other than serve the political base and its economic demands. But the moral questions raised by this system appear to have been largely ignored. Is Britain not the country which shouts loudest about its freedoms of thought and word? What a hollow claim that is when we look as closely as we have done at the men and women forged by the education system. What freedom have most of the young men and women of County High whose minds have been put in a straitjacket?

Not that I think County High is so very different from most other secondary schools – grammar, technical, modern, comprehensive – so these questions have relevance for the whole population. All educational institutions are ruled by a rigid centralised authoritarian structure which has shown itself less able to learn and slower to change than nearly all of its youngest components (i.e. infant pupils). County High is a disturbing microcosm.

I cannot carry further my thesis without reference to the school's teaching staff and its role. County High lacked what many other grammar schools had – a tradition. That is, it did not have a history which could influence its pupils, a grand past to overawe the newcomers and stimulate the elder forms. In no way did this deter the teachers from creating one themselves – an atmosphere plucked from their own grammar schools and universities and deposited in Dagenham. Instead of one specific culture in the school there were many individual versions. For instance, the traditional grammar school emphasis on character development was the concern of but a few teachers; rigorous discipline the domain of a few more; chatty informality the aim of others. Pupils learned to deal with separate styles, but none was stamped wholesale on the school. This diverse range of methods did not filter down to differences in the curriculum, which was set by the needs of teachers to get their pupils through examinations. Very few teachers encouraged classroom discussion, perferring instead the these-are-the-facts-now-go-away-and-learn-them approach. It is too simplistic to say that the boys and girls of County High were drilled in unquestioning obedience, but the school's failure to create a situation in which pupils could feel free to question and discuss greatly contributes to their undoubting outlook of life now. They are even unable to criticise the school on this level because they lack the critical faculties. It was a system which deprived the children of any incentive to speak their minds, participate in forming original ideas and thinking for themselves. Illich puts it so well. 'The safeguards of individual freedom are all cancelled in the dealings of a teacher with his pupil. When the schoolteacher fuses in his person the functions of judge, ideologue and doctor, the fundamental style of society is perverted by the very process which should prepare for life.' [3]

Limits were imposed by the need to assimilate facts for the sole purpose of repeating them on an examination paper. The total number of facts learned could be impressive and the record may look fine for the teacher who can boast that so many of his pupils in the past so many years have passed so many GCEs. It is proof positive of a teacher's ability and paper evidence to show the authorities that the job is being done. But such assessment of both pupil and teacher is crude. The teacher, given a free reign to guide pupils through their school careers without exam worries, with the aim only of opening up their minds, will not be able to produce paper evidence. Instead there will be a class of non-conformist, inquisitive, doubting and articulate human beings. Most probably they will also be angry, adaptable to change and anxious to achieve that change. One can understand that teachers – themselves products of the system they seek to perpetuate – are unprepared for this kind of education and that the present political system could not stand the upheaval. So there is an in-built bias to dissuade dissension. Even among staff not noted for their disciplinarian traits any challenge from pupils was frowned upon. I am not accusing the headmaster and the teaching staff of getting together and drawing up a formula for turning out obedient, unthinking office-boys and housewives. Any such idea is clearly ludicrous. Most of the teachers were as unaware of their collective role as were the children. If any teacher did analyse the problem, or even question the need for certain lessons and teaching methods, then the pupils were never made aware. Dissent among staff was never allowed to become common knowledge among the children. Dissent was the school's dirtiest word.

Many a liberal teacher will talk knowledgeably about the conflict between the State and its education machine. Speech days echo to well-modulated calls for change. Blueprints are mentioned, calling for a movement towards education that conveys only the basic essentials of information and then concentrates on stimulating pupils to think for themselves. Examinations are castigated. Schemes are expounded to rid schools of lessons – even teachers. Lip service is paid to every possible concept of educational reform. Fine words in many cases but better left unsaid if the speakers refuse to act. Surely those who understand one doctrine's failings and speak of alternatives, while continuing to work within the system, are more guilty than those who cannot comprehend any problem at all? The liberals' main failing is that the only way they see possible to administer a reformist remedy is by evolutionary change. For no matter how enlightened or radical teachers are, and these were categories I suspect were thinly distributed at County High, they can have little effect in bringing about fundamental changes in education. That is to not to say that I overlook the value of personal relationships with children, and the benefits of providing a happy atmosphere within a certain school. (Many of the interviewees said their days at school were happy enough.) But teachers' powers are localised and very limited.

Moreover, most teachers fifteen or so years ago in grammar schools were part of the middle class which has a stake in maintaining a stable political situation and even if they were not of that origin they had adopted middle class status. They did not question the society in which they lived, and which they were in a unique position to influence through the coaching of younger generations. At County High no one teacher can be apportioned more blame than the rest – they served the system in which they had been taught to believe and taught the children to believe as blindly. The majority fitted this mould, and what chance had the dissenters, if they existed, to change the school? The career structure rested on conformism after all. And according to the authorities, teachers' obligations were to make their pupils literate and numerate. 'Parents wouldn't like you to do anything else'; 'there's no money for extra facilities'; 'your job is not to question, not to subvert, it's to do the job.' And there is the nub of the matter. Even the so-called teachers' militancy displayed in recent years has been confined to the improvement of their own wages and conditions rather than to making moves to expose the system which rules their existence, and which requires them to inculcate their charges with the benefits of that code. Without necessarily realising they pass on intact to their pupils their own unquestioning obedience to authority. It is not surprising that schoolchildren, discouraged from asking questions, turn into adults with closed minds, without the mental training to overcome the processing. Schooling has prepared them for a certain place in the structure, perhaps a different lifestyle from their parents, but it has not imbued them with the capacity to challenge The System. Our schooling was simply a five-year course in how to succeed without understanding why.

At school the propaganda was subtle, but it combined well with the thrust from home. 'Pupils, you are in a privileged position; take your chances while you can; don't fall behind; don't end up like the secondary modern layabouts; there really is room at the top.' Classroom competition was fostered with the front-runners constantly exhorted to do better; and those at the bottom put under pressure to do much, much better. I hardly need add that the sports field was another element in the same indoctrination.

The school's influence over the children of County High could not have had so much impact unless the parents tacitly wished it to be so. Among middle class parents there has long been an understanding that education is important. Their wish for their children to succeed at school is therefore logical. For example, they may have encouraged them to have realistic expectations.

Most working class parents had not had a formal school education beyond the age of fourteen. Their youth had been interrupted by the Second World War, a war in which even if they did not take part they believed would lead to a new, more just and equal society. But the politicians' promises of the great egalitarian Britain in the late Forties and early Fifties were exposed as a dream by the time the children of this survey began their secondary school education. The fathers worked in factories, earning steady money, bought second-hand cars and boozed a bit at weekends. The mothers, if they escaped the house at all, worked in shops and canteens to help boost the family budget and buy 'extras', like holidays and Christmas presents. Dagenham was brutalising in its boredom. It was life. Their lot. But television showed them how 'the other half' enjoyed a better lot. Perhaps it was too late for them, but why should their children not enjoy the fruits of a better life? After all, weren't they going to a grammar school, 'getting educated'? If education does not result in upward mobility the working class consider it a waste of time. For the aspirant working class family, aspiring that is towards the secure middle class way of life which appeared to be a magnet for so much money, the push for the child to succeed was great. The only criterion for success in this atmosphere was money. 'You can do it, my son. Take all their learning. Work hard while you're young. Go into an office. Wear a suit to work. You'll be out of this hole in no time. There's coin at the top.' Disillusioned by the politics of future promise, degraded by the monotony of present work, dejected by the waste of past years the working class fathers presented to their children a portrait of lost hope. 'Put your faith in no one, boy. Not the politicians or the bosses or your neighbours. Go and grab all you can get now. It's the only way.' Individualism and avarice were unconsciously bred at the firesides of the Becontree Estate.

The boys of County High emerged into the adult world bursting with enthusiasm for little more than money. School and home, with good intentions but without analysis, had groomed a group of greedy graspers. (It would be unfair to conclude that the girls began work in the same spirit. Their indoctrination was of a different kind and I will discuss it later.) The once-favoured ideal that grammar schools would carry on the public school tradition of training for community service has been lost to the demands of industry and commerce, with its combatant spirit of competition and high monetary rewards. Only four people in this survey could lay claim to taking up a vocation – the husband and wife doing cancer research; the wife working as an occupational therapist; and one woman teacher. All questioned whether they had taken the right road because around them they can see others making money and living 'comfortable' lives. The other six teachers are involved in money-seeking. None of them see their job as a vocation, claiming that such a view is old-fashioned.

The search for money should be linked with the amazingly high incidence among the men of a wish to run their own businesses. Apart from the monetary rewards possible and the probable elevation in status, such a move must be seen as the result of parental pressure during schooldays and their own adult perception of society. They cannot face continuing wage slavery, even in managerial and executive positions. They cannot imagine themselves in twenty years' time as the disenchanted parents reciting to their children the bad luck stories they heard from their own fathers. Being their own bosses would eliminate any chance of similarity in their own eyes. At the other end of the scale, among the more content men without the urge to try their hand at running a business, is a relatively early acceptance of their new lot. This generally occurs when a promotional ladder meets their aspirations; or if they have already achieved a great deal more than their fathers.

Routes to the top of the earning tree, or to the point where they can branch out themselves, may appear on the surface to have been haphazard, but close inspection shows a desire to 'do better' in stages. Each job move has been made in the hope of better monetary prospects in the future. Community service forms no part in the majority of career structures. The jobs have won their takers good wages – good, that is, in comparison with the wages of their fathers and good in that all are above the agreed national earnings average at the time of writing. Most are well over the norm. This money has enabled the men to buy houses and cars and stereo record players and colour televisions and automatic washing machines and many other items considered luxuries by their parents and essentials by them to maintain their own standards within their new community. The pride of acquiring material possessions is obvious. They have collected money and consumer goods and houses like so many adult GCEs. I also detected a genuine concern for the well-being of the family unit – the wife and, in the relevant cases, the children. But the conditioning process has narrowed these young men's horizons so that rarely could I discern signs of love for fellow man. The fight to succeed at school, the propagandising of the home, the competitive climb up the office promotional ladder, the lack of political consciousness had combined to produce capitalism's contented servant, an individualistic go-getter. For want of a better phrase these men are uncharitable. Not in the financial sense, of course, but in their opinions and dealings with people from outside their restricted world. Wrapped in nuclear family domesticity inside a mortgaged house bedecked with electric gadgetry there is a sort of siege mentality. Not having had such an environment in their childhood; amazed at the affluent turn of their fortunes and unable to pin-point the reasons for it; unsure of the future they are inclined to treat outsiders with suspicion.

They suspect the motives of people who work for little reward. 'There must be something in it for them,' said one. 'Social workers and youth club leaders and that sort, they're a funny lot,' said another. 'They put in loads of work and they don't get much money. It doesn't make sense. Who cares? And it doesn't do them any good.'

They suspect immigrants. Numerous examples of naked racism apart, many men are concerned with what they believe to be the economic threat of the black worker. Others dislike the import of a different culture.

They suspect intellectualism. Having been trained at school to accept facts and to regurgitate them later they lack the capacity for discussion. Argument is not part of their culture. Serious reading is a rarity, so there is always a lack of information. Philosophical and religious debate is almost unknown. Indeed, on one occasion a wife butted into my conversation with her husband to say: 'We have a rule in this house. You can talk about anything except politics and religion. They're banned. They always lead to arguments.' The husband nodded in agreement.

They suspect political change. This can be traced directly to their fathers' disillusion in some cases. For most it is a sincerely-held belief that anything which threatens the status quo must, of itself, be wrong.

They deny the existence of a class structure. For almost all, class is something which does not have relevance. It may have done once, but not now. They see differences in society in simple and subjective terms: there are the worse-off, who are unlucky or work-shy and the better-off, who are lucky – i.e. inherited wealth – or work hard. They do not speak of themselves as middle class and cannot see that the change in their lifestyle from childhood to the present has led to their *embourgeoisement.* They seem suspended in limbo, a class void.

These many suspicions are not often articulated. They are assumed by the men in the groups in which they mix. This situation means that the men are both uncharitable and complacent. They surround themselves with people of a like mind and there is no challenge to their way of life. Incidentally, they do not appear to be motivated by the sort of 'them and us' envy of their parents' generation, believing that everything they reasonably need is attainable in a society which has given them material rewards early in life. Happy at home, secure at work, reinforced in friendship the stage is set for apathy. At 26 years of age there is a lamentable lack of understanding and vision. They are what human beings become when they trade life for existence and ambition for security.

In the section in which I dealt with working class women I outlined how home background influenced the girls to play the traditional, subordinate roles in relation to men. The success of that instruction can be seen in that few remain independent in their adult lives. The majority have married and a third spend their time looking after children at home. Most working wives assume that they will end up as housewives.

Unlike the men most women are relatively unworried about making big money. They enjoy all the material benefits provided by money and revel in the security of their homes but their application to the philosophy of making money is weaker than that of their male peers. They share the siege mentality, however, and indeed show a greater tendency to suspect 'outsiders'. The women are less competitive and less ambitious and far more apathetic than the men. Many of them talked as though they have achieved liberation while they patently have not, seeming to revel in the self-delusion. They mislead themselves into believing that they are liberated because they sometimes refuse to take the dog for a walk. Although women enter less into the forefront of the capitalist rat race they condone it, supporting perhaps their husbands in their promotional ambitions, or helping their bosses wage their office power games. Again there is a failure to question and to analyse. There is acceptance of rule and role.

The new class

The affluence, attitudes and apathy of the men and women who graduated from County High has placed them, for want of a better description, in a class all of their own. The middle class have marked time. Upward mobility of sorts has carried the working class away from their childhood status. They have said goodbye to the working class. Their values have altered and they are inclined to be embarrassed by the continuing link through their parents. However, they have not joined the varied middle classes. (Given that the term 'middle class' is subjective in the extreme, and that it is perhaps nothing more than socio-economic shorthand, there is nevertheless an amorphous group which refers to itself as middle class. Definition of middle class is therefore almost impossible from the outside because the middle class exists only in the minds of those who lay claim to be part of it.) My contemporaries do not call themselves middle class. They are wedged into the structure so that they form part of a new class — what I will call the 'domesticated class.' This is not to say that I overlook the 'domestication' of the working class and those people who want to be called middle class. I am merely attempting to name this new phenomenon of the class in a void.

The Cuban revolutionary leader, Fidel Castro, speaking of his own education, said: 'That was the time when they did not teach one to think, but forced one to believe. I am of the opinion that when man's ability to think and reason is impaired he is turned from a human being into a domesticated animal.'[4]

I believe, on the weight of evidence I have discovered, that this is an apposite comment on the education offered at County High and in Dagenham's homes. The emergence of the 'domesticated class' is another of capitalism's crimes against humanity. In the country which allows capitalism all excesses, the United States, the late black revolutionary George Jackson wrote: 'The school systems are gauged to teach youth what to think, not how to think.' [5]

In Britain, Anthony Arblaster, writing about the lack of real freedom in higher education, has written: 'Students are ... being told *what* they ought to think about for themselves, and very often *how* they ought to think about it as well.' [6]

We are churning out from our schools more and more unthinking, docile recruits to a vast 'domesticated class.' They form a distinct sub-culture, which is as different from that of their working class childhood as it is from the present so-called middle classes. The new class, which has blurred the once black-and-white class divisions, embraces a design for living which 'borrows' certain styles from both, yet it is distinctive enough to be noticeable to the members of either the working or middle class. These 'differences' include language, aspirations, religious and political beliefs and leisure activities. The working class will claim that their offspring have moved into the middle class by virtue of their private houses, their new voting allegiance and their status at work. The middle class will make many contradictory statements to deny these newly-affluent young people a place in their ranks. Some may say that they earn too much, others that they earn too little. That they think only of money but do not spend it wisely; that they are uncultured; that their speech is 'common'; that they lack taste in house furnishing, perhaps, or clothing or entertainment. There will be criticism of their 'bringing down' the neighbourhood. Truly, most of the arguments will be based on snobbery for that is the hallmark of the middle class. The schism is thus acknowledged by the settled classes. One characteristic only appears to be shared between the 'domesticated class' and the middle classes in large measure, and that is their political apathy.

What part does Dagenham play in this transformation from working class to domestication? I believe the Becontree Estate to be for many the first step out of the working class, especially for those who arrive very young and whose parents provide an environment in which their children are likely to achieve at school. Working class families transported from London's East End on to the Estate often set their sights on giving their children 'the chance I never had'. For the children of County High there was a chance to escape from their fathers' tedious daily toil and so they moved out from Dagenham at the first chance (usually marriage), away from the working class area into rural Essex, into enclaves of the 'domesticated class', by which I mean the little private estates.

Obviously the children who go on to university stand a better chance of escaping this vicious circle but Dagenham is a notoriously difficult area from which to go on to higher education – even now. Eric Midwinter, co-director of the Advisory Centre for Education, drew up in 1973 a league table of 103 towns where children stood the best and worst chances of higher education. The Borough of Barking, which includes Dagenham, was ninety-seventh in that list.[7]

Willmott would have us believe that it's all because of the lack of social mix. He wrote: 'There is no doubt in my mind that education at Dagenham suffers from the estate's social uniformity. Schools in mixed-class districts benefit from the enthusiasm and stimulation of middle class parents and their children, who help to create an atmosphere which can be stimulating . . .'[8]

Social mix may get a few more to university, it might make school a more life-enhancing process for some pupils, but it will not end the indoctrination. School in Dagenham, as elsewhere, will continue to fail to open the young minds. Unless the basis of education itself is changed completely schools will continue to help 'domesticate' children.

There are those interviewees who do not conform to the pattern of the 'domesticated class'. Firstly, the ten with middle class parents appear to have settled themselves into the middle class. Nine have done so without any apparent understanding of the class structures, and are as mindless in many respects as those I have described in the previous sections of this chapter. The tenth, a university lecturer, is a self-confessed liberal intellectual. Among the working class sample, six of the men lead lives very much like those of their parents, except that they are relatively affluent. And one major difference: there is little evident pride in being working class. A seventh, the drop-out, enjoys the political kudos of his working class upbringing, but his rejection of society stems, in my opinion, from personality problems which lay outside arguments over stratification. Among the working class women there are eight who have married within the working class and who lead traditional working class female existences. Movements on the social scale, if any, have been too slight to record in any of these cases. They have remained static and they do differ in certain respects of behaviour and life style from the 'domesticated class'.

The middle class interviewees are less ambitious and present pictures of stability, security and lack of anxiety. The male working class interviewees are inclined to be more angry about inequality – as evidenced by the incidence of Communist sympathy – but are pessimistic about the chances of change. The working class females revealed a them-and-us philosophy – i.e. *them* have it and *us* don't – which is akin to the attitude I discovered among working class parents. They are also apathetic. To sum up, I consider that most of the men and women who remain working class have been what they would regard as 'unlucky'. Given half a chance I suspect they would still like to climb out of the working class.

However, it is not the static alone who do not conform to the 'domesticated class' tag. There are two working class women who do not fit the description, the cancer researcher and one teacher. They display a working knowledge of Britain's political system and its alternatives, and understand the complexities of modern life. They both have open and questioning minds. I also wonder at my own situation in this respect, and without attempting to over-simplify the varying pressures I attempted to discover similarities between the three of us. I noted that we were encouraged to be independent by our parents, that we left home immediately upon leaving school and that we did not return home again. But others who followed a similar pattern emerge differently so that trying to find a common cause proved worthless, and while I am in a good position to write at length about my own reasons for overcoming the system I cannot about the others. Suffice it to say instead that by a freak of good fortune, perhaps by the law of averages, we have won through. This prompts me to ask: is it right that a system exists in which only a tiny fraction can survive the brainwashing?

My research has not uncovered anything that has not been revealed many times before. Sociologists have produced a prolific collection of material on the problems of educational inequality, although they have been less vigilant in their approach to the end results of British education, equal or not. There is a widely held belief that changes within the system can improve it. One of the main results of the Plowden Report, which highlighted the causal link between social deprivation and poor academic achievement at primary school level, was the creation of Educational Priority Areas where a policy of 'positive discrimination' was introduced to end the vicious circle.[9] Briefly, money was made available in these areas to improve education: various community school projects were started; pre-schooling was encouraged; financial inducements were made to stop the turn-over in teaching staff; changes in curriculum were attempted. This action was guided by a research team directed by A. H. Halsey, who was to write with great insight on the problems facing teachers in our unbalanced society. After completing the first chapter of *Educational Priority* he wrote: 'I have been arguing that if we seriously intend to create a society of equal and participating democrats we have to begin with fundamental economic and political reforms. A more equal distribution of wealth and income which is, and is seen to be, fair. A devolution of political power including power over education . . .' [10]

Dr. Halsey, aware of this need for a revolutionary transfer of power and wealth, argues that reforms are possible within the system, in spite of educational reformism's poor past record. Reform is an illusion, the social-democratic sop which allows the present system to continue its bad, old habits while promising a future of hope and enlightenment. In making equality of education the key issue he also overlooks the problem of the emerging adult trained as a child under our system. It is not surely his intention that we should achieve a situation in which all British school-children are equally domesticated?

The reformist's attitude plays into the hands of the rulers of a system which has designed schooling to perpetuate generations of super consumers dedicated to the divisive doctrine of fierce competition in a society taught to venerate economic growth. The exploiters are hardly likely to sit back and allow wide-ranging reforms if they can prevent, or harass, them. Mao Tse-tung noted this very point in 1920. He wrote:

'Education requires (i) money, (ii) people, and (iii) instruments. In today's world, money is entirely in the hands of the capitalists. Those who have charge of education are all either capitalists or slaves of capitalists. In today's world, the schools and the Press, the two most important instruments of education, are entirely under capitalist control. In short, education in today's world is capitalist education. If we teach capitalism to children, these children, when they grow up, will in turn teach capitalism to a second generation of children. Education thus remains in the hands of the capitalists.' [11]

What Mao recognised 55 years ago was that to attempt educational reforms within the system was a waste of effort.

'If one wishes to use the power of education to transform

them (capitalists), then since one cannot obtain control of the whole or even an important part of the two instruments of education – the schools and the Press – even if one has a mouth and a tongue and one or two schools and newspapers as a means of propaganda ... this is really not enough to change the mentality of the adherents of capitalism even slightly ... '

Mao went on to conclude that 'capitalism cannot be overthrown by the force of a few feeble efforts in the domain of education'.

And it is the revolution Mao was then advocating for his country which I insist is now the only way forward for ours. It is scandalous that so many people over so long a period can merely ask for 'a just society'. In Britain there is a tradition – more prevalent in education, perhaps, than elsewhere – that all change must be slow to be good. Every new idea must be old before it is implemented. Evolutionary advance in education means that millions of children suffer under a system which leading educationists know to be wrong. No reformist passive offensive within this system brings forth a fundamental change. Only a revolution can stop the criminal intellectual castration of children in this country carried out in the name of freedom of thought, word and action. What freedom is it to speak at Hyde Park Corner when the listeners have numbing preconceptions which prevent them understanding a 'new' point of view? What freedom is it to own a house and a car and a blank mind? What freedom is it to work within a system without understanding how the system works? County High's 'domesticated class' do not have the freedom of thought to even ask those questions.

Our capitalist educational system stands accused of hypocrisy and inhumanity – the former because it claims to be free but patently is not, and the latter because it is in some measure aware of its shortfalls yet makes no real effort to overcome them. The lesson is clear: to achieve freedom we must have a new system. If capitalism will not of its own accord welcome the introduction of a free-thinking society then the first step must be to conclude this system.

Notes

Part One

Subliminal schooling

1. *The Outline of History* (Chapter 40 of the 1951 edition).
2. *Early Leaving Report* (1954).
3. Floud, Halsey and Martin, *Social Class and Educational Opportunity* (1956) p. 114.
4. B. Jackson and D. Marsden (1962, Revised 1966).
5. Plowden Report: *Children and their Primary Schools* (1967).
6. Jackson and Marsden (1966) p. 16.

Landscape for a Working Class

1. *The Guinness Book of Records* describes the Becontree Estate as the largest in the U.K. It gives no world classification.
2. *A company's story in its setting, Samuel Williams and Sons Ltd., 1855-1955,* R. Sinclair.
3. *Becontree and Dagenham* (1934) T. Young. According to the GLC, the weekly rent for a three-room house on the Estate in 1928 was 10s 3d (roughly 51p). It was twice reduced and until 1953 the rent was 7s 9d (39p). There have been regular rent rises ever since.
4. A further complication in discussing Dagenham is that in 1965, under GLC reorganisation, Dagenham Borough was merged in what was termed 'a shotgun marriage' with Barking and took the latter name for its single-borough title.
5. *Evolution of a Community,* P. Willmott, p.38. Although unattributed by Willmott the quote is from Leslie Cannon, the then deputy borough librarian of Dagenham.
6. The now retired Mr O'Leary, described by many as an eccentric, impressed me on the few occasions I met him with his ebullient, hearty self-confidence. He loved Dagenham and defended it often, sometimes by scholarly argument and on other occasions with an emotional outburst. He also wrote two books about the area, *The Book of Dagenham* and *Dagenham Place Names.*

7. The latest Ford of Dagenham employment figures are 28,000. This decline is due to the greater use of automation and a policy of decentralisation. Ford's now have five other centres in Essex alone.
8. *The Cameron Report* (1957).
9. *The Jack Report* (1963).
10. *Working for Ford* (1973) H. Beynon, p. 59.
11. No doubt excluding Peking! Mr Cannon can be forgiven his hyperbole. It may not be true today, but in the 40s and 50s it is probable that he is literally correct.
12. See also Willmott, op. cit., pp. 86-140.
13. Willmott, op. cit., pp. 87-88.
14. Wickford is a mid-Essex bungaloid suburb some twenty miles from Dagenham.
15. In spite of Dagenham being smokeless this was a recurring comment.

High school, or low?

1. *The Grammar Schools – Their Continuing Tradition 1660-1714,* W. A. L. Vincent, p. 93.
2. Mr Grainger was still headmaster when County High was dissolved in 1970 when the Borough of Barking introduced its system of comprehensive education. The building is still standing and forms part of a three-school complex known as Parsloes-Manor Comprehensive School.
3. It was pitiful to hear when I visited the school that the library had been turned into a staffroom and the books piled in a storeroom.
4. Fourteen boys and one girl said they were caned, the boys on the bottom and the girls on the hand. Six boys had the punishment more than once. Several boys were caned on the last day of their school lives for a farewell prank. It is also interesting to note that of the 15 caned, 13 were in the C or D streams.
5. *The Sociology of Education,* P. W. Musgrave, p. 156.

Part Two

Middle class perpetuation

1. Jackson and Marsden (1966), op. cit., pp. 42-46.
2. 'The council' was the local colloquial name for the fenced area of grass at the corners of roads on the Becontree Estate. The name possibly originated from the noticeboard in the centre of the green which said that ball games were banned and ended with the words: 'By order of the Council.'
3. I offered him the addresses of two but he said: 'We've probably lost all we had in common. To make contact now might break that memory.'
4. Abbs Cross Technical School was situated in Hornchurch. As a technical school it was ranked below a grammar.
5. If this were really so then eight graduates out of 122 was a poor result for such a policy.
6. See the chapter entitled 'Nasty Habits'.
7. Dudley Moore was the County High boy who made good, winning a music degree at Oxford and fame as a satirist, jazz musician, television and film star.

Divided we learn

1. Willmott, op. cit., p. 17.
2. Willmott, op. cit., pp. 65-66.
3. Jackson and Marsden, op. cit., pp. 67-70.
4. It was not until the Education Act of 1944 that the school leaving age was raised to fifteen.
5. Triptons was a secondary modern school in Dagenham.
6. Because this was the strongest clique, as mentioned previously, it was the most attractive or most repulsive according to differing viewpoints.
7. This is not a wayward thought, for secondary modern schools in the area did achieve amazing results with small groups of pupils each year.
8. A sophisticated form of noughts and crosses.
9. I have dealt separately with this girl in the chapter entitled Lonely Victims.
10. Another of the Lonely Victims.
11. See Note 7 above.
12. Jim Sanger was the only person in the survey who had a parent

with first-hand knowledge of County High, his mother having been one of its first pupils.

13. No grandiose mansion this, but a cottage near the Thames marshes for a factory supervisor.

United we earn

1. One has definitely made the trip, having since written to me from Perth.
2. Two were not earning when I carried out the interviews. One was a student and the other had opted out. He is another in the Lonely Victims chapter.
3. See Lonely Victims.
4. See Page 112.
5. The father was a local government employee who acted as a mayoral aide.
6. *Social Mobility and Political Change,* I. Davies, p. 18.
7. This council accommodation was unique in that it was on a private estate. The man in question worked as an officer for the local council.
8. Three more teachers fall into the working category.
9. The inference being that the fifth form monitors were cruel to their charges. While all first formers, particularly the boys, suffered from bullying there was no evidence of lunch time starvation.
10. This is the girl forced to do homework in the garden shed and refused permission to stay on for sixth form studies.
11. The Conservative Government's Industrial Relations Bill which was later enacted, and later still, was repealed by the Labour Government.

Lonely Victims

1. Jean's leaving became a scandal of some interest for several weeks after she had gone. Rumours and ill-natured gossip revived months later when the baby was born. A couple of girls visited her for a while, and one of those girls still sees Jean regularly now.

'Nasty Habits'

1. *Barking Record No 70* (January 1966) Written by Leslie Cannon.
2. The Post Office found it necessary to install a Dagenham Exchange in 1953 due to demand. It opened with 689 subscribers. By 1961 there were 6,500 telephones linked to the exchange. One of the most valuable assets in my tracking down of the interviewees was the fact that so many of their parents were, or had been, on the telephone.
3. See *Social Class, Language and Education,* D. Lawton for a critique of research on speech and literacy by Professor Basil Bernstein.
4. *Fowler's Modern English Usage,* Oxford University Press (1965), p. 356.
5. For the purposes of this section I have not included myself, but if the reader uses the 122 sample figure then I too should be added to the literary list.
6. A term, now out of fashion, to describe a Dexamyl pill, a combination of amphetamine and barbiturate.
7. The famous Old Bailey trial between Penguin Books and the Crown took place in November 1960.
8. Since smoking was a 'crime' for which pupils were caned it is impossible to know whether the punishment was administered for smoking alone or for masturbation as well.
9. I have omitted the schoolgirl pregnancy from this group.
10. Mrs Mary Whitehouse is secretary of the National Viewers and Listeners Association, a body of her own creation dedicated to the preservation of her own moral code.

Part Three

The Domesticated Class

1. *Success and Failure in the Secondary School,* O. Banks and D. Finlayson, p. 3.
2. Musgrave (1972), op. cit., p. 329.
3. *Deschooling Society,* I. Illich, p. 31.
4. Castro speaking in Havana in 1961. Entitled Words to the Intellectuals and reprinted in *Radical Perspectives in the Arts,* Editor: Lee Baxandall.

5. Letter to his mother dated March 12, 1965 from *Soledad Brother: The Prison Letters of George Jackson.*
6. *Academic Freedom,* A. Arblaster, p. 16.
7. This fact, attributed to Dr Midwinter, was quoted in the *Daily Mirror* of April 12, 1973. The article, about social and educational inequalities, was headlined 'To have and to have not.'
8. Willmott, op. cit., p. 115.
9. *Educational Priority Vol. 1,* A. H. Halsey, p. vii.
10. Quote from an article headlined 'EPA go away . . . come again another day' in *The Guardian* of December 4, 1973.
11. Quoted from the extracts of two letters to Ts'ai Ho-sen in November 1920 and January 1921, published in *Hunan Li-shih Tzu-liao* No. 9, 1959. Translated by Stuart Schram in *The Political Thought of Mao Tse-tung,* pp. 296-7.

Appendix

Ask a person what makes him tick and the chances are that he will retreat into his shell. Discovering what a person thinks, how he lives and why he thinks and lives the way he does is never easy. However, I had a big advantage in this study because I knew many of the people and shared their background, education and upbringing. This knowledge gave me a head start when I set out to ask them scores of personal questions. In consequence, the questionnaire I used usually formed a basis for conversation, and I believe I culled as much information from random talks as I did in the statistics from questions. I often changed the sequence, changed the wording and prompted answers by adding explanations.

This is a run-down of the basic questionnaire. I began by checking names, ages, whether they were married, had children, and what sort of house they lived in. Was it on a mortgage or rented? Did they work and what was their salary? Did they drive and own a car?

The following section related to schooldays. Which stream were they in? When did they leave and why? Did they enjoy their schooldays? If they had misgivings or grumbles we talked about them. How did they feel about discipline? Did they behave badly – receiving detentions or the cane? Were they in any trouble outside school? When the time came to leave were they sad or was it a relief? Had they found school a stimulating experience? What were their GCE exam results?

Which languages had they learned – and did they speak them now? How much had they joined in school activities – the debating society, choir, plays, sports teams etc? Did they enjoy games lessons? What was their attitude to examinations? Did they feel under stress – from teachers or their parents? Did any teacher especially influence them? And did they keep in touch with any teacher after leaving?

Did they go to church while at school – and do they go now? How would they describe their religious affiliation or outlook now? And if they have changed, when and why? Did they consider religious education a necessary subject to to be taught at school? Should current affairs have formed a bigger part of the curriculum? Would sex education have been beneficial?

Did they make many friends at school? Who did they mix with

and why? How did they feel in relation to other pupils – inferior, superior, better off, happier etc? Had they kept in touch? Did they ever go out on a date with another pupil? Did they ever have a crush on a teacher? Did they ever smoke, or take drugs, at school – and since? Did they read widely – and now? What was their attitude to the school uniform? Did they receive careers advice, and did they have any special ambition? What part did their parents play in their attention to schoolwork? How did they get on with their parents? Was there any friction in the house? Had they brothers and sisters? Did they go to County High? What do they do? What did they think of the headmaster? And the teaching staff? Did they consider the facilities adequate? Overall, did they think they had a good education?

What did they think of Dagenham? For those living outside, I asked them for a comparison with their own area.

Then came a brief summary of their lives since leaving school, starting with any educational attainments. How many jobs had they had, why had they changed, what influenced them? I tried to obtain as much information as possible on their main turning points – jobs, marriage, housing etc. Had they ever worked for Ford, or had any member of their family? What was their father's job? Mother's job? What was their parents' background and education? Did they find living with their parents oppressive, if they still lived with them? If not, how different was life now in comparison with the parental home? And turning to the present, I asked first about their work. Do they enjoy it? How many people work under them, if at all? I asked them to explain their position in the firm, and their career hopes. Did they feel under any stress? Did they feel they had made any mistakes? Are they union members?

How had marriage come about? (If unmarried, why not?) Did they consider getting married was inevitable? What kind of school did their partner come from, and which area? How did they meet? Was their relationship different from that of their parents? On many occasions the partner was present and these questions, particularly, prompted them to join in. Did they have many friends? Where were they drawn from? How did they spend their social life? Did they have any special interests or hobbies? Did they play sport? Did they belong to any clubs? Were they members of the library? Did they belong to book clubs? Which magazines did they read, and which newspapers? Why? Did they have a TV and was it a colour set? (Furniture generally was noted, and I was often given a tour of 'the new house'.) Did they drink? Where had they

176

been on holiday? Did they go on holiday as a child? Comparisons were made between childhood and present.

A link was made to the question about sex education. I then asked if their parents had taught them about sex. If not, how had they learned about the sex act? Did they consider that the best, or healthiest, way of learning? Were they offended by 'dirty' jokes at school? Did they understand contraception by the time they came to leave school? Did they ever experiment sexually while of school age? When did they first have intercourse? Did they marry the person concerned? What did they think of the so-called permissive society? What were their attitudes to censorship?

A link was made to the question on current affairs at school, and classroom discussions. Were they particularly interested in politics? Had they ever voted – and for which party? Why did they vote for that party? What was their attitude towards trades unions? What did they think of the Industrial Relations Act? Were they conscious as children of Ford's industrial disputes? Did their fathers ever go on strike? Did they consider themselves as working (middle) class as children? Which class did they think fitted them now? What were their attitudes to race relations? (I mentioned the name of Enoch Powell to most of the interviewees.) Were they happy about the present political system? Would they like to see a change? To what?

How would they like to see their own children educated? Did they like the comprehensive school plan?

Lastly, I asked them if they had any hopes, dreams or ambitions. I also asked them if they thought I had covered their lives in my questions? Did they think I had missed anything out?

Bibliography

Arblaster, A., *Academic Freedom,* (Penguin Education/Council for Academic Freedom and Democracy, 1974).

Banks, O. and Finlayson, D., *Success and Failure in the Secondary School,* (Methuen, 1973).

Baxandall, Lee, (ed.), *Radical Perspectives in the Arts,* (Pelican, U.S.A., 1972).

Beynon, H., *Working For Ford,* (Allen Lane, 1973).

Cameron Report, Report of a Court of Inquiry, (HMSO, 1957).

Davies, I., *Social Mobility and Political Change,* (Macmillan, 1970).

Early Leaving, (HMSO, 1954).

Floud, J., Halsey, A. H., and Martin, F. M., *Social Class and Educational Opportunity,* (Heinemann, 1956).

Halsey, A. H., and others, *Educational Priority, Vol. One,* (HMSO, 1972).

Illich, I., *Deschooling Society,* (Calder & Boyars, 1971).

Jack Report, Report of a Court of Inquiry, (HMSO, 1963).

Jackson, B. and Marsden, D., *Education and the Working Class,* (Pelican Books Revised edition, 1966).

Jackson, G., *Soledad Brother,* (Jonathan Cape/Penguin Books, 1971).

Lawton, D., *Social Class, Language and Education,* (Routledge and Kegan Paul, 1968).

Musgrave, P. W., *The Sociology of Education,* (Methuen, Revised edition, 1972).

O'Leary, J. G., *The Book of Dagenham,* (Dagenham B.C., 1964).

Plowden Report: Report of the Central Advisory Council for Education, *Children and their Primary Schools,* (HMSO, 1967).

Sinclair, R. and others, *A company's story in its setting, Samuel Williams & Sons Ltd, 1855-1955,* (Samuel Williams & Sons, Ltd.).

Schram, S. R., *The Political Thought of Mao Tse-tung,* (Penguin Books, Revised edition, 1969).

Vincent, W. A. L., *The Grammar Schools – Their Continuing Tradition 1660-1714,* (Murray, 1969).

Wells, H. G., *The Outline of History,* (Cassell, Revised edition, 1951).

Willmott, P., *The Evolution of a Community: A study of Dagenham after forty years,* (Routledge & Kegan Paul, 1963).

Young, T., *Becontree and Dagenham: A report made for the Pilgrim Trust,* (London, Becontree Social Survey Committee, 1934).

Index

181

Index